DOCTRINA NOVAE HIEROSOLYMAE
DE SCRIPTURA SACRA /
TEACHING OF THE NEW JERUSALEM
CONCERNING SACRED SCRIPTURE

DOCTRINA
NOVAE HIEROSOLYMAE
DE SCRIPTURA SACRA

AB
EMANUEL SWEDENBORG

EDITED BY JOHN ELLIOTT

LONDON
THE SWEDENBORG SOCIETY
2019

TEACHING OF THE NEW JERUSALEM CONCERNING SACRED SCRIPTURE

BY

EMANUEL SWEDENBORG

TRANSLATED BY JOHN ELLIOTT

LONDON
THE SWEDENBORG SOCIETY
2019

Published by the Swedenborg Society
Swedenborg House, 20-21 Bloomsbury Way, London WC1A 2TH

© Swedenborg Society 2019

Cover artwork: Stephen McNeilly
Typeset in Palatino at Swedenborg House
Printed and bound in Great Britain
at TJ International, Padstow

ISBN 978-0-85448-213-9

British Library Cataloguing-in-Publication Data
A catalogue record for this book
is available from the British Library

CONTENTS

Editor and Translator's Introduction	page vii
Abbreviations	xi
Doctrina Novae Hierosolymae de Scriptura Sacra	2
Teaching of the New Jerusalem concerning Sacred Scripture	3
Table of Parallel Passages	175

EDITOR AND TRANSLATOR'S INTRODUCTION

Doctrina Novae Hierosolymae de Scriptura Sacra (SS) is the second of the seven works published by Emanuel Swedenborg in Amsterdam during the second half of 1763 and the first month or two of the following year. A second edition of the Latin text appeared in 1835 and a third in 1889, further details of which are given below, on page xi. Thus the Latin text in the present two-language publication constitutes a fourth edition. The accompanying English version however follows many previous translations and revisions produced in the past two and a half centuries; details of these will be found in the soon-to-be published fourth volume of **A Descriptive Bibliography of the Works of Emanuel Swedenborg** 1688-1772 (**RB**), edited and compiled by Norman Ryder.

No lengthy introduction to this new edition of **SS**, Latin and English, is called for, since much that could be said has been stated already in my Editor and Translator's Introduction to the recently published two-language edition of **Doctrina Novae Hierosolymae de Domino (DD)**, the first of 'the Amsterdam Seven'. Just a few things need to be mentioned here.

Relation to Apocalypsis Explicata
Written in 1762 and/or early 1763, **SS** is in part a re-working of certain sections of **Apocalypsis Explicata (AE)**, the long work Swedenborg was producing in preceding years but never completed and therefore never published. These sections in **AE** are spread out below §§1066-1089, ie underneath the explanations of verses 10-17 of chapter 17 of the Book of Revelation.

Relation to Prophets and Psalms
In **SS** Swedenborg refers explicitly, in §113, to his having read all through the prophetical books Isaiah-Malachi and the Book of Psalms, though he does not mention that, as he went along, he had been making brief notes on the spiritual level of meaning in them.

His brief explanation, at the end of §97 in **SS**, of the first chapter of Ezekiel is clearly a revised wording of the notes he had made on that chapter in **Prophets and Psalms (PP)** – the English title given to a manuscript found among Swedenborg's books and papers after his death. And in §§85-87 of **SS** his 'blocks' of quotations from Isaiah-Malachi and the Psalms seem to spring from his close reading of these books in the Old Testament and his God-given perception of their inner or spiritual meaning.

Relation to Schmidt's Latin Version of the Bible

When Swedenborg was quoting Sacred Scripture he relied generally on Sebastian Schmidt's Latin version, first published in 1696 in Strasbourg. The system of versification adopted by Schmidt however, and therefore by Swedenborg, varies in many places from that found in English versions of the Bible. The placement, in the present two-language edition of **SS**, of Latin text and English translation alongside each other allows those chapter-and/or-verse variations to be easily identified.

Relation to Vera Christiana Religio

Chapter Four of **Vera Christiana Religio (VR)** – published by Emanuel Swedenborg in Amsterdam in 1771 – is largely a revision of **SS**. As far as possible I have endeavoured, in the English version of **SS**, to reproduce the late John Chadwick's translation of **VR**, which first appeared in print in 1988.

Divine Name

In most English versions of the Old Testament the Hebrew Divine name which was never uttered, called the Tetragrammaton, is rendered as the LORD; but in his Scriptural quotations in which that name occurs Swedenborg has **Jehovah** or occasionally **Jehovih**. For more on this matter, please see my Editor and Translator's Introduction to **DD**.

Editorial Decisions regarding the Latin Text

With one exception, Swedenborg's Neo-Latin spelling of words has been retained (that exception being the employment by his printers in Amsterdam of the *ae* diphthong instead of the *oe*). But the use of capitals, italics, punctuation, and so on, found in the first Latin edition has generally been abandoned and more modern conventions followed instead; and most Roman numerals have been altered to Arabic. Swedenborg's careful 'highlighting' of words or

phrases within quotations from Sacred Scripture, which was not retained by the editor of the third Latin edition, nor consequently by translators relying on that text, has been restored.

Acknowledgements
My consultant has again been Revd Robert Gill, who I must again thank for his sound judgment and careful attention to detail in the editing of the Latin text and translating of it, and in the provision of critical apparatus and editorial notes.

Also, I wish to thank again Revd Norman Ryder for supplying me with information prior to its appearance in volumes yet to be published of **RB**;[1] Stephen McNeilly and James Wilson for seeing to the proper layout of Latin text and critical apparatus on left-hand pages, and English translation and footnotes on right-hand ones; and Judy my wife for her constant love and support. And above all, Gratias Domino!

London 2015   *John Elliott*

---

[1] Norman Ryder sadly passed away in July 2018 having submitted the files for volumes four and five of **RB** for publication. These volumes are forthcoming, to be published by the Swedenborg Society

ABBREVIATIONS

Works cited in Editor and Translator's Introduction and footnotes

RB	**A Descriptive Bibliography of the Works of Emanuel Swedenborg (1688-1772)** edited and compiled by Norman Ryder; published by the Swedenborg Society Volume One 2010 (repr. 2017); Volume Two 2012; Volume Three 2015; Volume Four in preparation
AE	**Apocalypsis Explicata** Unfinished work, published after Swedenborg's death
AR	**Apocalypsis Revelata** All editions
AR^1	**Apocalypsis Revelata** First edition, 1766
AR^2	**Apocalypsis Revelata** Second edition, 1881, editor Samuel H Worcester
DD	**Doctrina Novae Hierosolymae de Domino** All editions
PP	**Summaria Expositio Sensus Interni Librorum Propheticorum et Psalmorum** Published after Swedenborg's death
SS	**Doctrina Novae Hierosolymae de Scriptura Sacra** All editions
SS^1	**Doctrina Novae Hierosolymae de Scriptura Sacra** First edition, 1763
SS^2	**Doctrina Novae Hierosolymae de Scriptura Sacra** Second edition, 1835, editors L Hofaker and G Werner
SS^3	**Doctrina Novae Hierosolymae de Scriptura Sacra** Third edition, 1889, editor Samuel H Worcester
VR	**Vera Christiana Religio** All editions

*VR*¹ **Vera Christiana Religio**
First edition, 1771
*VR*² **Vera Christiana Religio**
Second edition, 1857, editor JFI Tafel
*VR*³ **Vera Christiana Religio**
Third edition, 1889, editor Samuel H Worcester

DOCTRINA NOVAE HIEROSOLYMAE
DE SCRIPTURA SACRA /
TEACHING OF THE NEW JERUSALEM
CONCERNING SACRED SCRIPTURE

Doctrina Novae Hierosolymae de Scriptura Sacra

Quod Scriptura Sacra seu Verbum sit ipsum Divinum Verum

1   In omnium ore est quod Verbum sit a Deo, divinitus inspiratum et inde sanctum, sed usque hactenus nescitum est ubinam in eo Divinum est, nam Verbum in litera apparet sicut scriptum vulgare, stylo peregrino, non sublimi nec lucente sicut ad apparentiam sunt scripta saeculi. Ex eo est quod homo qui naturam pro Deo, aut qui illam prae Deo, colit – et inde ex se et suo proprio, et non e caelo a Domino – cogitat, facile in errorem de Verbo, et in contemtum ejus, possit cadere, et secum dicere cum id legit, Quid hoc? quid illud? an hoc est Divinum? an Deus, cui infinita sapientia est, ita loqui potest? ubi et unde sanctum ejus, nisi ex religioso, et inde persuasione?

2   Sed qui ita cogitat, ille non considerat quod Ipse Jehovah, qui est Deus caeli et terrae, loquutus sit Verbum per Mosen et Prophetas, et quod inde non possit esse quam ipsum Divinum Verum, nam quod Ipse Jehovah loquitur, hoc illud est. Nec considerat quod Dominus, qui est idem cum Jehovah, loquutus sit Verbum apud Evangelistas, multa ex Suo ore et reliqua ex spiritu oris Sui, qui est Spiritus Sanctus. Inde est quod Ipse dicat quod in verbis Suis sit vita, et quod Ipse sit lux quae illustrat, et quod sit Veritas.

Quod Ipse Jehovah loquutus sit Verbum per Prophetas, ostensum est in **Doctrina Novae Hierosolymae de Domino**, n.52,53. Quod verba quae Ipse Dominus apud Evangelistas loquutus est vita sint, apud Johannem,

Verba quae Ego loquor vobis, spiritus sunt, et vita sunt, 6:63.

Apud eundem,

Teaching of the New Jerusalem concerning Sacred Scripture

Sacred Scripture, that is, the Word, is Divine Truth itself

1   Everyone professes the Word to be from God, divinely inspired and therefore holy, but up to the present no one has known where in it the Divine is. For taken literally the Word looks like any ordinary book, written in a strange style, neither high-flown nor brilliant as many secular books appear to be. This is why if people worship nature as God or in preference to God, so that their thought comes from self and what is their own rather than from heaven inspired by the Lord, they can easily fall into error about the Word and come to despise it. Thus they say to themselves when they read it, What does this or that mean? Can this be Divine? Can God, whose wisdom is infinite, talk like this? Where is there anything holy in it, and where does this holiness come from, except from religious belief and the conviction it carries?

2   People who think like this fail to reflect that Jehovah Himself, who is the God of heaven and earth, uttered the Word by means of Moses and the Prophets, and consequently it cannot be anything but Divine Truth itself. For this is what everything is that Jehovah Himself speaks. They fail too to reflect that the Lord, who is the same as Jehovah, uttered the Word in the Gospels, much of it from His own lips, and the remainder from the spirit of His mouth, which is the Holy Spirit. This is why He Himself says that His words contain life, and that He is the light that enlightens, and that He is the truth.

That Jehovah Himself uttered the Word by means of the Prophets has been shown in **Teaching of the New Jerusalem concerning the Lord,** §§52-53; and that the words which the Lord Himself uttered in the Gospels are life He declares in John,

The words which I speak to you are spirit, and they are life. 6:63.

In the same gospel,

Jesus dixit mulieri ad fontem Jacobi, Si scires donum Dei, et quis sit qui dicit tibi, Da Mihi bibere, tu peteres ab Eo, et daret tibi aquam viventem. Qui bibit ex aqua quam Ego dabo non sitiet in aeternum; sed aqua quam Ego dabo ei fiet in eo fons aquae salientis in vitam aeternam. 4:6,10,14.

Per fontem Jacobi significatur Verbum; ut quoque Deut.33:28, quare etiam Dominus ibi sedit, et loquutus est cum muliere; et per aquam significatur verum Verbi. Apud eundem,

Jesus dixit, Si quis sitiverit, venito ad Me et bibito. Quisquis credit in Me, sicut dicit Scriptura, Flumina e ventre illius fluent aquae viventis. 7:37,38.

Apud eundem,

Petrus dixit ad Jesum, Verba vitae aeternae habes. 6:68.

Quare Dominus dicit apud Marcum,

Caelum et terra transibunt; verba Mea non transibunt. 13:31.

Quod verba Domini sint vita, est quia Ipse est vita et veritas, ut docet apud Johannem,

Ego sum via, veritas, et vita. 14:6.

Et apud eundem,

In principio erat Verbum, et Verbum erat apud Deum, et Deus erat Verbum. In Illo vita erat, et vita erat lux hominum. 1:1,4.

Per Verbum ibi intelligitur Dominus quoad Divinum Verum, in quo solo vita est et lux est. Ex eo est quod Verbum, quod a Domino et quod est Dominus, dicatur fons aquarum vivarum, Jer.2:13; 17:13; 31:9; fons salutis, Esai.12:3; fons, Sach.13:1; ac fluvius aquae vitae, Apoc.22:1; et dicitur quod Agnus, qui in medio throni, pascet illos, et deducet illos ad vivos fontes aquarum, Apoc.7:17. Praeter aliis in locis, ubi Verbum etiam vocatur sanctuarium et tabernaculum in quo Dominus habitat cum homine.

Jesus said to the woman at Jacob's well, If you knew the gift of God, and who it is who says to you, Give Me a drink, you would ask Him, and He would give you living water. Those who drink of the water that I shall give will never thirst; but the water which I shall give them will become a well of water springing up in them to eternal life. 4:6,10,14.

Jacob's well means the Word, as it also does in Deut.33:28. That too is why the Lord sat down there and talked to the woman. And water means the truth of the Word. In the same gospel,

Jesus said, If any are thirsty, let them come to Me and drink. Whoever believe in Me, as the Scripture says, Streams of living water will flow from their belly. 7:37,38.

In the same gospel,

Peter said to Jesus, You have the words of eternal life. 6:68.

The Lord therefore says in Mark,

Heaven and earth will pass away; My words will not pass away. 13:31.

The reason why the Lord's words are life is that He is life and truth, as He teaches in John,

I am the way, truth, and life. 14:6.

And in the same gospel,

In the beginning was the Word, and the Word was with God, and the Word was God. In Him was life, and the life was the light of people. 1:1,4.

The Word here means the Lord in respect of Divine Truth, in which alone there is life and light. This is why the Word, which is from the Lord and is the Lord, is called a spring of living waters, Jer.2:13; 17:13; 31:9; a spring of salvation, Isa.12:3; a spring, Zech.13:1; and a river of the water of life, Rev.22:1; and it is said that the Lamb, who is in the midst of the throne, will feed them and bring them to living springs of water, Rev.7:17. There are other places too where the Word is called a sanctuary and tabernacle in which the Lord dwells with people.

3   Sed homo naturalis ex his usque non persuaderi potest quod Verbum sit ipsum Divinum Verum, in quo Divina Sapientia est et Divina Vita, spectat enim illud a stylo, in quo non videt illa. Sed stylus Verbi est ipse stylus Divinus, cum quo omnis alius stylus, utcunque sublimis et excellens apparet, non comparari potest, est enim sicut caligo ad lucem. Stylus Verbi talis est ut sanctum sit in omni sensu, inque omni voce, imo alicubi in ipsis literis; inde Verbum conjungit hominem Domino et aperit caelum.

Sunt duo quae procedunt a Domino, Divinus Amor et Divina Sapientia seu, quod idem, Divinum Bonum et Divinum Verum, nam Divinum Bonum est Divini Amoris Ipsius et Divinum Verum est Divinae Sapientiae Ipsius. Verbum in sua essentia est utrumque hoc; et quia illud conjungit hominem Domino et aperit caelum, ut dictum est, ideo Verbum implet hominem qui illud a Domino, et non a semet solo, legit, bono amoris et veris sapientiae – voluntatem ejus bono amoris et intellectum ejus veris sapientiae. Inde homini est vita per Verbum.

4   Ne itaque homo in dubio esset quin Verbum tale sit, revelatus mihi est a Domino sensus internus Verbi, qui in sua essentia est spiritualis, qui sensui externo, qui est naturalis, inest, sicut anima corpori. Ille sensus est spiritus qui vivificat literam, quare ille sensus potest de Verbi divinitate et sanctitate testari, et convincere etiam hominem naturalem, si vult convinci.

3   But those who think on only a natural level still cannot be convinced by these quotations that the Word is Divine Truth itself, containing Divine Wisdom and Divine Life, because they look at it from the point of view of its style, and in this they cannot see these things. However, the style of the Word is the actual style of God, with which no other style, however high-flown and magnificent, can be compared, for it is like thick darkness in contrast to light. Such is the style of the Word that there is holiness in every sentence, every word, in some places even every letter. Thus the Word forms a link between a person and the Lord, and opens the way to heaven.

There are two things which proceed from the Lord, Divine Love and Divine Wisdom, or in other words Divine Goodness and Divine Truth since Divine Goodness consists in His Divine Love, and Divine Truth in His Divine Wisdom. The Word is in its essence both of these; and because it forms a link between a person and the Lord and opens the way to heaven, as I have said, the Word therefore fills people – those who read it with the Lord's aid and do not rely on self alone – with the goodness of love and the truths of wisdom. It fills their will with the goodness of love, and their understanding with the truths of wisdom. This is how a person has life by means of the Word.

4   Therefore to prevent people from doubting what the Word is like the Lord has revealed to me the internal sense of the Word, which in its essence is spiritual. This is present within the external or natural sense like the soul within the body. That sense is the spirit which gives life to the literal form. Consequently that sense can bear witness to the divinity and holiness of the Word, and convince even those who think on only a natural level, if they are willing to be convinced.

Quod in Verbo sensus spiritualis sit, hactenus ignotus

Haec in hoc ordine dicenda sunt −

i   Quid sensus spiritualis
ii   Quod ille sensus in omnibus et singulis Verbi sit
iii   Quod ex illo sit quod Verbum divinitus inspiratum sit, ac in omni voce sanctum
iv   Quod ille sensus hactenus ignotus fuerit
v   Et quod non alicui posthac detur nisi qui in genuinis veris a Domino est

5   i **Quid sensus spiritualis.** Sensus spiritualis non est ille qui ex sensu literae Verbi elucet, quando quis scrutatur et explicat Verbum ad confirmandum ecclesiae quoddam dogma; hic sensus est sensus Verbi literalis. Sed sensus spiritualis non apparet in sensu literae; est intus in illo, sicut anima in corpore, sicut cogitatio in oculis, et affectio in facie, quae unum agunt ut causa et effectus. Ille sensus imprimis facit ut Verbum sit spirituale, non modo pro hominibus sed etiam pro angelis, quare Verbum per illum sensum communicat cum caelis.

6   A Domino procedit **Caeleste**, **Spirituale**, et **Naturale**, unum post alterum. **Caeleste** dicitur quod procedit ex Divino Amore Ipsius, et est Divinum Bonum; **Spirituale** dicitur quod procedit ex Divina Sapientia Ipsius, et est Divinum Verum; **Naturale** est ex utroque; est illorum complexus in ultimo. Angeli regni caelestis Domini, ex quibus est tertium seu supremum caelum, sunt in Divino quod procedit a Domino, quod caeleste vocatur, nam sunt in bono amoris a Domino. Angeli regni spiritualis Domini, ex quibus est secundum seu medium caelum, sunt in Divino quod procedit a Domino,

The Word contains a spiritual sense unknown up to the present

Aspects of this will be discussed in the following order –

i   What the spiritual sense is
ii   This sense is present in every part and detail of the Word
iii   It is this which makes the Word divinely inspired and holy in every word
iv   This sense has up to the present been unknown
v   It will in future only be granted to those who are in possession of genuine truths from the Lord

5   i **What the spiritual sense is.** The spiritual sense is not the one which transparently underlies the literal sense of the Word, when it is scrutinized and expounded by anyone to support some dogma of the church; this is the literal sense of the Word. But the spiritual sense is not to be seen in the literal sense; it lies within it, like the soul in the body, thought in the eyes, or affection in the face, which act in unison as cause and effect. This sense is the chief reason why the Word is spiritual, not only for people in the world but also for the angels. This is why this sense enables the Word to act as a channel of communication with the heavens.

6   From the Lord there proceed that which is **Celestial**, that which is **Spiritual**, and that which is **Natural**, one after the other. The term **Celestial** is given to that which proceeds from His Divine Love, and is Divine Goodness; the term **Spiritual** is given to that which proceeds from His Divine Wisdom, and is Divine Truth; what is **Natural** comes from both of these, being their totality at the outermost level. The angels of the Lord's celestial kingdom, who make up the third or highest heaven, are in the Divine called the celestial which proceeds from the Lord, for they are in possession of the goodness of love coming from the Lord. The angels of the Lord's spiritual kingdom, who make up the second or middle heaven, are in the Divine called the spiritual which proceeds from the Lord,

quod spirituale vocatur, sunt enim in veris sapientiae a Domino.* Homines autem ecclesiae in mundo, sunt in Divino naturali, quod etiam procedit a Domino. Ex his sequitur quod Divinum procedens a Domino ad ultima sua descendat per tres gradus, ac nominetur Caeleste, Spirituale, et Naturale. Divinum quod a Domino ad homines descendit, per tres illos gradus descendit, et cum descenderat, tres illos gradus in se continet. Omne Divinum tale est; ideo quando est in suo ultimo gradu, est in suo pleno. Tale est Verbum. Hoc in ultimo suo sensu est naturale, in interiori est spirituale, ac in intimo est caeleste; et est Divinum in unoquovis. Quod Verbum tale sit, non apparet in sensu literae ejus, qui est naturalis, ex causa quia homo mundi antehac non sciverat aliquid de caelis, et inde non quid spirituale, et quid caeleste, ita nec discrimen inter illa et inter naturale.

7   Discrimen inter hos gradus nec sciri potest nisi sciatur correspondentia; nam tres illi gradus inter se prorsus distincti sunt, sicut finis, causa, et effectus, aut sicut prius, posterius, et postremum, at unum faciunt per correspondentias; naturale enim correspondet spirituali, et quoque caelesti. Quid autem correspondentia, videri potest in opere **De Caelo et Inferno**, ubi actum est De Correspondentia omnium Caeli cum omnibus Hominis (n.87-102); et De Correspondentia Caeli cum omnibus Telluris, n.103-115; et amplius videbitur ab exemplis e Verbo infra adducendis.

8   Quoniam Verbum interius est spirituale et caeleste, ideo per meras correspondentias conscriptum est, et quod scriptum est per meras correspondentias, hoc in sensu ultimo scriptum est tali stylo, quali apud Prophetas et apud Evangelistas, qui tametsi apparet vulgaris, usque ille sapientiam Divinam et omnem angelicam in se recondit.

9   ii **Quod sensus spiritualis in omnibus et singulis Verbi sit**, non melius videri potest quam ab exemplis, quae sint haec sequentia. Dicit Johannes in Apocalypsi,

---

*   [Author's footnote] Quod duo regna sint, ex quibus caeli consistunt, quorum unum vocatur Regnum Caeleste, alterum Regnum Spirituale, videatur in opere **De Caelo et Inferno**, n.20-28

for they are in possession of the truths of wisdom coming from the Lord.* But the people who make up the church in the world are in the Divine natural, which too proceeds from the Lord. From all this it follows that the Divine proceeding from the Lord down to its lowest limits passes through three degrees, called Celestial, Spiritual, and Natural. The Divine coming down from the Lord to people passes through those three degrees, and having done so holds those three within itself. Everything Divine is like this, and therefore when it resides in its lowest degree it does so in its fullness. It is so with the Word. In its outermost sense it is natural, in its more inward sense spiritual, and in its inmost sense celestial; and it is Divine in each of these. But this, the nature of the Word, is not evident in its literal, that is, natural sense, for the reason that up to now people in the world have not known anything about the heavens, or therefore what the spiritual is and what the celestial is, and so have not known, either, about the difference between each of these and what is natural.

7   Nor is it possible to know the difference between these degrees without a knowledge of correspondence, for these three degrees are entirely distinct and separate from one another, like end in view, cause, and effect, or first in order, next in order, and last in order. They make one however through correspondences, for natural corresponds to spiritual, and also to celestial. But what correspondence is may be seen in the work **Heaven and Hell**, where the subject is *Everything in heaven has a correspondence with something in people*, §§87-102, and *Everything in heaven has a correspondence with something on earth*, §§103-115; and more will be seen in the examples quoted below from the Word.

8   Since the Word is inwardly spiritual and celestial nothing else than correspondences have therefore been used in the composition of it; and what has been written with the use of nothing else than these has been written in its outermost sense in the kind of style that exists in the Prophets and the Gospels. This style, although it seems to be ordinary, nevertheless conceals Divine and all angelic wisdom within itself.

9   ii **The spiritual sense is present in every part and detail of the Word**. This can be seen best from examples, such as the following. John says in the Book of Revelation,

---

*   [Author's footnote] The heavens consist of two kingdoms, one of which is called the Celestial Kingdom, the other the Spiritual Kingdom, see the work **Heaven and Hell**, §§20-28

Vidi caelum apertum, cum ecce! equus albus; et qui Sedens super eo vocabatur Fidelis et Verus, qui in justitia judicat et pugnat. Et oculi Ejus sicut flamma ignis, ac super capite Ejus diademata multa; habens nomen scriptum, quod nemo scit nisi Ipse. Et indutus erat vestimento tincto sanguine; et vocatur nomen Ipsius **Verbum Dei**. Exercitus Ejus in caelo sequebantur Ipsum super equis albis, induti byssinum album et mundum. Habet super vestimento et super femore Suo nomen scriptum, **Rex regum et Dominus dominorum**. Vidi porro unum angelum stantem in sole, qui clamavit voce magna, Venite et congregamini ad caenam magnam, ut comedatis carnes regum, et carnes chiliarchorum, et carnes fortium, et carnes equorum et sedentium super illis, et carnes omnium liberorum et servorum, et parvorum et magnorum. 19:11-18.

Quid haec significant, nemo videre potest nisi ex sensu spirituali Verbi, et nemo sensum spiritualem nisi ex scientia correspondentiarum, nam omnes voces sunt correspondentiae, et nulla vox ibi est vana. Scientia correspondentiarum docet quid significat equus albus et quid Sedens super illo, quid oculi qui sicut flamma ignis, quid diademata quae super capite, quid vestimentum tinctum sanguine, quid byssinum album quo induti qui ab exercitu Ipsius in caelo, quid angelus stans in sole, quid caena magna ad quam venirent et congregarentur, tum quid carnes regum, et chiliarchorum, et plurium aliorum, quas comederent.

      Quid autem singula in sensu spirituali significant, videatur in opusculo **De Equo Albo**, ubi explicata sunt, quare illa ulterius explicare hic supersedetur. Ostensum est in illo opusculo quod Dominus quoad Verbum ibi describatur, et quod per oculos Ipsius qui sicut flamma ignis, et per diademata quae super capite, et per nomen quod nemo scit nisi Ipse, intelligatur sensus spiritualis Verbi, et quod nemo illum sciat nisi Ipse Dominus, et cui Ipse vult illum revelare; tum quod per vestimentum tinctum sanguine intelligatur sensus naturalis Verbi, qui est sensus literae ejus, cui violentia illata est. Quod sit Verbum quod ita describitur, manifeste patet, nam dicitur, **Vocatur nomen Ejus Verbum Dei**; et quod sit Dominus qui intelligitur, etiam manifeste patet, nam dicitur quod nomen Sedentis super equo scriptum sit, **Rex regum et Dominus dominorum**.

    3   *om* sicut *SS, VR*

I saw heaven open, and behold! a white horse; and He who sat on it was called Faithful and True, and in righteousness He judges and fights. And His eyes were like a flame of fire, and on His head were many diadems. He had a name written, which no one but He knows. And He was clothed in a garment dyed in blood; and His name is called **The Word of God**. His armies in heaven followed Him on white horses, clothed in linen white and clean. He has written on His garment and on His thigh a name, **King of kings and Lord of lords**. I saw further an angel standing in the sun, who cried in a loud voice, Come and gather to the great supper, to eat the flesh of kings, and the flesh of captains, and the flesh of strong men, and the flesh of horses and of those that sit on them, and the flesh of all free men and slaves, both small and great. 19:11-18.

No one can see what all this means except from the spiritual sense of the Word, and no one can see this sense except by knowing the correspondences. For every word corresponds to something; not one word there lacks a meaning. A knowledge of correspondences shows the meaning of white horse and Him who sat on it, eyes which were like a flame of fire, diadems which were on His head, garment dyed in blood, white linen which was worn by His army in heaven, angel standing in the sun, great supper which they were to come and gather to, as well as flesh of kings, and captains, and many more which they were to eat.

The meanings in the spiritual sense of these details may be seen where they have been set out in the small work **The White Horse**, so there is no need to say anything more about them here. In that small work it was shown that this passage in the Book of Revelation is describing the Lord as the Word. His eyes which were like a flame of fire, the diadems which were on His head, and the name which no one but He knows serve to mean the spiritual sense of the Word, which no one knows except the Lord Himself and those He wants to reveal it to. It was also shown that garment dyed in blood means the natural sense of the Word, that is, its literal sense, to which violence was done. It is quite plain that it is the Word which is so described, for it says, **His name is called The Word of God**; and it is also quite plain that it is the Lord who is meant, for it says that the name written of Him who sat on the horse is **King of kings and Lord of lords**.

Quod sensus spiritualis Verbi aperiendus sit in fine ecclesiae, significatur non modo per illa quae de equo albo et de Sedente super illo nunc dicta sunt, sed etiam per caenam magnam, ad quam per angelum in sole stantem omnes invitati sunt ut venirent ac ederent carnes regum et chiliarchorum, fortium, equorum, sedentium super illis, omnium liberorum et servorum. Omnes hae expressiones forent voces vanae, et absque vita et spiritu, nisi spirituale intus in illis esset, sicut anima in corpore.

10 In Apocalypsi, cap. 21, describitur ita Sancta Hierosolyma, quod in illa esset luminare simile lapidi pretiosissimo, sicut lapidi jaspidi, instar chrystalli splendenti. Quod haberet murum magnum et altum, habentem portas duodecim, et super portis angelos duodecim, et nomina scripta duodecim tribuum filiorum Israelis. Quod murus esset 144 cubitorum, quae est mensura hominis, hoc est, angeli, et quod structura muri esset jaspis, et fundamenta ejus ex omni lapide pretioso, ex jaspide, sapphiro, chalcedonio, smaragdo, sardonyche, sardio, chrysolitho, beryllo, topazio, chrysopraso, hyacintho, et amethysto. Quod duodecim portae essent duodecim margaritae. Quod ipsa civitas esset aurum purum, simile vitro puro et quod esset quadrangularis; longitudo, latitudo, et altitudo essent aequales, 12000 stadiorum; praeter plura. vers.11,12,16-21.

Quod omnia haec spiritualiter intelligenda sint, constare potest ex eo quod per Sanctam Hierosolymam significetur nova ecclesia quae a Domino instauranda est, ut in **Doctrina de Domino**, n.62-65 ostensum est. Et quia per Hierosolymam ibi significatur ecclesia, sequitur quod omnia quae dicuntur de illa ut civitate, de portis ejus, de muro ejus, de fundamentis muri, tum quae de mensuris eorum, sensum spiritualem contineant, nam illa quae ecclesiae sunt, spiritualia sunt. Quid autem singula significant, in opere **De Nova Hierosolyma** – Londini, anno 1758, edito – n.1, explicatum est, quare ulterius illa explicare supersedeo. Satis est ut inde sciatur quod sensus spiritualis insit singulis descriptionis ejus, ut anima corpori, et quod absque illo sensu nihil ecclesiae intelligeretur in illis quae ibi scripta sunt, ut, quod civitas esset ex puro auro, portae ejus ex margaritis, murus ex jaspide, fundamenta muri ex lapidibus pretiosis, quod murus esset 144 cubitorum, quae mensura hominis, hoc est, angeli; quod ipsa urbs esset longitudine,

2   albo VR: om SS

The disclosure of the spiritual sense of the Word at the end of the church is what is meant not only by what has just been said about the white horse and Him who sat on it, but also by the great supper to which the angel standing in the sun invited all to come to eat the flesh of kings and captains, strong men, horses, those that sit on them, all free men and slaves. All these expressions would be meaningless, devoid of life and spirit, if they did not have an inner spiritual content, like the soul within the body.

10   In the Book of Revelation, chapter 21, the Holy Jerusalem is described as having a source of light like a most precious stone, similar to the jasper stone, shining like crystal. It had a great and high wall with twelve gates, and twelve angels above the gates, and the names inscribed of the twelve tribes of the children of Israel. The wall was 144 cubits, which is the measure of a person, that is, an angel. The material of the wall was jasper, and its foundations of every precious stone, jasper, sapphire, chalcedony, emerald, sardonyx, sardius, chrysolite, beryl, topaz, chrysoprase, jacinth, and amethyst. The twelve gates were twelve pearls. The city itself was pure gold, resembling clear glass; and it was four-square, its length, breadth, and height were equal, 12000 stades[1], and other details, 21:11,12,16-21.

All this must be understood spiritually, as is evident from the fact that the Holy Jerusalem means the new church which is to be founded by the Lord, as has been shown in **Teaching concerning the Lord**, §§62-65. And since Jerusalem there means the church it follows that everything which is said of the city, its gates, its wall, foundations of the wall, as well as their measurements, contains a spiritual sense, for anything that relates to the church is spiritual. The meanings of these details have been laid out in §1 of the work **The New Jerusalem**, published in London in 1758, so I do not need to say anything more about them here. It is enough to know from this that the details of the description contain a spiritual sense, as the body does a soul. Without that sense nothing of what is written there could be understood as referring to the church, for instance, that the city was of pure gold, its gates were of pearls, the wall was of jasper, the foundations of the wall were of precious stones, the wall was 144 cubits, which is the measure of a person, that is, an angel; and

---

1   ie about 1350 miles. The stade was an ancient measure of length, roughly 170 metres

latitudine, et altitudine 12000 stadiorum, et plura. Qui autem ex scientia correspondentiarum sensum spiritualem novit, is intelligit illa, ut quod murus et fundamenta ejus significent doctrinam ex sensu literali Verbi, et quod numeri 12, 144, 12000 similia significent, nempe omnia vera et bona ecclesiae in uno complexu.

11 In Apocalypsi, cap.7, dicitur quod 144000 obsignati essent, 12000 ex unaquavis tribu Israelis; totidem ex tribu Jehudae, ex tribu Rubenis, Gadis, Ascheris, Naphtali, Menassis, Simeonis, Levi, Jisascharis, Zebulonis, Josephi, et Benjaminis. Sensus spiritualis horum est quod omnes apud quos ecclesia a Domino est salventur, in spirituali enim sensu per signari in frontibus, seu obsignari, significatur agnosci a Domino et salvari. Per duodecim tribus Israelis significantur omnes ab illa ecclesia; per 12, 12000, et 144000, omnes, per Israelem ecclesia, et per unamquamvis tribum aliquod specificum ecclesiae. Qui hoc illorum verborum spirituale non scit, opinari potest quod solum tot salvandi sint, et illi modo a gente Israelitica et Judaica.

12 In Apocalypsi, cap.6, dicitur quod cum Agnus aperuit primum sigillum libri, exiret equus albus, et quod sedens super illo haberet arcum, cui data est corona. Quod cum aperuit secundum sigillum, exiret equus rufus, et quod sedenti super illo data esset machaera magna. Quod cum aperuit tertium sigillum, exiret equus niger, et quod sedens super illo in manu teneret stateram. Et quod cum aperuit quartum sigillum, exiret equus pallidus, et quod nomen sedentis super illo esset Mors.

Quid haec significant, solum per sensum spiritualem potest evolvi; et plene evolvitur dum scitur quid significat aperitio sigillorum, quid equus, et quid reliqua. Per illa describuntur successivi status ecclesiae quoad intellectum Verbi, a principio ad finem ejus. Per aperitionem sigillorum libri ab Agno significatur manifestatio illorum statuum ecclesiae a Domino; per equum intellectus Verbi. Per equum album intellectus veri ex Verbo in primo ecclesiae statu, per arcum sedentis super illo equo doctrina charitatis et fidei pugnans contra falsa, per coronam vita aeterna victoriae praemium.

Per equum rufum significatur intellectus Verbi deperditus quoad bonum in secundo ecclesiae statu, per machaeram

that the city itself was 12000 stades in length, breadth, and height, and so forth. But anyone who knows the spiritual sense from a knowledge of correspondences can understand these statements, as for instance, the wall and its foundations mean the teaching derived from the literal sense of the Word, and the numbers 12, 144, 12000 have a similar meaning, that is, all of the church's truths and forms of goodness taken together.

11   In the Book of Revelation, chapter 7, it says that 144000 were sealed, 12000 from each tribe of Israel – the same number from the tribe of Judah, Reuben, Gad, Asher, Naphtali, Manasseh, Simeon, Levi, Issachar, Zebulon, Joseph, and Benjamin. The spiritual meaning of this is that all those with whom the church that comes from the Lord resides are saved, for to be marked with the seal on their foreheads, or to be sealed, means to be accepted by the Lord and to be saved. The twelve tribes of Israel stand for all who are part of that church – 12, 12000, and 144000 meaning all, Israel meaning the church, and each tribe some specific feature of the church. Anyone unacquainted with this spiritual content of these words may suppose that only that actual number are to be saved, and these from merely the Israelite and Jewish nation.

12   In the Book of Revelation, chapter 6, it says that when the Lamb opened the first seal of the book a white horse came out, and that he sitting on it had a bow, to whom was given a crown. When He opened the second seal a red horse came out, and to him sitting on it was given a large sword. When He opened the third seal a black horse came out, and he sitting on it held a balance in his hand. And when He opened the fourth seal a pale horse came out, and the name of him sitting on it was Death.

The meaning of all this can be unfolded only with the aid of the spiritual sense; and it is unfolded fully when one knows what an opening of seals means, what horse means, and what every other detail means. These images serve to describe the consecutive stages of the church, from start to finish, so far as its understanding of the Word is concerned. The opening of the seals of the book by the Lamb means the revealing by the Lord of those stages of the church; a horse means the understanding of the Word. The white horse means an understanding of truth derived from the Word in the first stage of the church; the bow of him sitting on that horse means the teaching of love and faith fighting false ideas, while his crown means eternal life, the reward for victory.

The red horse means an understanding of the Word in which good has been lost in the second stage of the church; the large

magnam falsum pugnans contra verum. Per equum nigrum significatur intellectus Verbi deperditus quoad verum in tertio ecclesiae statu, per stateram aestimatio veri tam parva ut vix aliqua. Per equum pallidum significatur intellectus Verbi nullus ex malis vitae et inde falsis in quarto seu ultimo ecclesiae statu, et per mortem damnatio aeterna. Quod talia in sensu spirituali per illa significentur, non apparet in sensu literae seu naturali, quare nisi sensus spiritualis semel aperiretur, Verbum quoad hoc, et quoad reliqua in Apocalypsi, foret clausum, adeo ut tandem nullus sciret in quo Sanctum Divinum ibi lateret. Pariter quid significatur per quatuor equos et per quatuor currus exeuntes ab inter duos montes aeris, apud Sachariam 6:1-8.

13   In Apocalypsi, cap.9, legitur,

Quintus angelus clanxit, et vidi stellam e caelo delapsam in terram, et data ei clavis putei abyssi. Et aperuit puteum abyssi, et ascendit fumus ex puteo sicut fumus fornacis magnae; et obscuratus est sol et aer ex fumo putei. Et e fumo exiverunt locustae in terram, et data est illis potestas, sicut habent potestatem scorpii terrae. Figurae locustarum similes equis paratis ad bellum; et super capitibus illarum sicut coronae similes auro, et facies illarum sicut facies hominum. Et habebant capillos sicut capillos mulierum, et dentes earum sicut leonum erant, Et habebant thoraces sicut thoraces ferreos; et vox alarum illarum sicut vox curruum equorum multorum currentium in bellum. Et habebant caudas similes scorpiis, et aculei erant in caudis illarum, et potestas illarum laedere homines mensibus quinque. Et habebant super se regem, angelum abyssi; nomen ei Hebraice Abaddon, in Graeca nomen habet Apollyon.

Haec nec ullus intellecturus esset nisi ei revelatus esset sensus spiritualis, nam nihil ibi inaniter dictum est; omnia quoad singula significant. Agitur ibi de statu ecclesiae, quando omnes cognitiones veri ex Verbo deperditae sunt, et inde homo sensualis factus persuadet sibi quod falsitates sint veritates.

    Per stellam e caelo delapsam significantur cognitiones veri deperditae; per solem et aerem obscuratum significatur lux veri caligo facta; per locustas quae e fumo putei illius

23   thoraces sicut SS^3 : om SS^1, SS^2
24   alarum SS^3 : om SS^1, SS^2
24   om equorum SS

sword means falsity fighting against truth. The black horse means an understanding of the Word in which truth has been lost in the third stage of the church; the balance means a valuation of truth so small as to be scarcely any at all. The pale horse means no understanding of the Word because of evil ways of life and consequent false ideas in the fourth or final stage of the church, and death means eternal damnation. That such things are meant in the spiritual sense by these images is not evident in the literal or natural sense, and therefore without the opening up at some time of its spiritual sense the Word so far as this description and everything else in the Book of Revelation are concerned would be a closed book, so much so that at length no one would know where the Divine holiness lay in it. The same goes for what is meant by the four horses and four chariots coming out from between the two mountains of bronze, in Zechariah 6:1-8.

13   In the Book of Revelation, chapter 9, we read,

The fifth angel sounded, and I saw a star fallen from heaven to earth, and there was given to him the key of the bottomless pit. And he opened the bottomless pit, and smoke rose from the pit like the smoke of a great furnace; and the sun and the air were darkened with the smoke of the pit. And from the smoke there came out locusts onto the earth, and power was given to them like the power scorpions of the earth have. The shapes of the locusts were like horses prepared for war, and on their heads there were as if crowns resembling gold, and their faces were like human faces. And they had hair like women's hair, and their teeth were like lions' teeth. And they had breastplates like breastplates of iron, and the noise of their wings was like the noise of chariots of many horses running into battle. And they had tails like scorpions, and the stings were in their tails, and their power to hurt people for five months. And they had a king over them, the angel of the bottomless pit; his name in Hebrew is Abaddon, and in Greek he has the name Apollyon.

Nor would any understand all this unless the spiritual sense had been revealed to them, for nothing stated there is meaningless; every single detail has some meaning. The subject there is the state of the church, when all awareness of truth derived from the Word has been lost, and as a consequence people who have come to rely solely on their senses convince themselves that falsities are truths.

2   Star fallen from heaven means recognitions of truth that were no longer known; sun and air darkened means the light of truth that has become thick darkness; locusts which came out of the

exiverunt significantur falsa in extremis, qualia sunt illis qui sensuales facti sunt, et omnia vident et judicant ex fallaciis; per scorpium significatur persuasivum eorum. Quod locustae apparuerint sicut equi parati ad bellum, significat ratiocinationes illorum sicut ex intellectu veri; quod locustis coronae similes auro super capite fuerint, et quod facies illarum sicut facies hominum, significat quod apparerent sibi sicut victores et sapientes; quod illis capilli sicut capilli mulierum, significat quod apparerent sibi sicut in affectione veri essent; quod illis dentes sicut leonum, significat quod sensualia, quae sunt ultima naturalis hominis, apparerent illis sicut in potentia super omnia; quod illis thoraces sicut thoraces ferrei, significat argumentationes ex fallaciis per quas pugnant et valent; quod illis vox alarum sicut vox curruum equorum multorum currentium in bellum, significat ratiocinationes sicut a veris doctrinae ex Verbo, pro quibus pugnandum; quod illis caudae sicut scorpiis, significat persuasiones; quod illis aculei in caudis, significat astutias fallendi per illas; quod illis potestas laedendi homines mensibus quinque, significat quod in aliquem stuporem inducant illos qui in intellectu veri et in perceptione boni sunt; quod haberent super se regem, angelum abyssi, cui nomen Abaddon aut Apollyon, significat quod falsa illorum essent ab inferno, ubi mere naturales, et in propria intelligentia.

  Hic illorum verborum sensus spiritualis est, ex quo non aliquid apparet in sensu literae. Simile est ubivis in Apocalypsi. Sciendum est quod in sensu spirituali omnia cohaereant in continuo nexu, ad quem concinnandum unaquaevis vox in sensu literae seu naturali conducit. Quare si vocula auferretur, nexus rumperetur et copula periret; ideo, ne id fieret, in fine hujus libri prophetici adjectum est quod non auferretur verbum, Apoc.22:19. Simile est cum libris Prophetarum Veteris Testamenti, e quibus ne aliquid auferretur; ex Divina Providentia Domini factum est ut singula in illis usque ad literas numerata essent, hoc a Masoretis.

14 Ubi Dominus de consummatione saeculi, quae est ultimum tempus ecclesiae, coram discipulis Suis loquitur, ad finem praedictionum de successivis status mutationibus ejus, dicit,

---

14-15 *om* equorum multorum SS

smoke of that pit mean false ideas on outermost levels, like those that people possess who have come to rely solely on their senses, seeing and judging everything with notions that are delusions; scorpion means the ability of those false ideas to be convincing. The locusts looking like horses prepared for war means their reasonings that seem to spring from an understanding of what is true; the locusts having crowns resembling golden ones on their head, and their having faces which were like human faces, means that they seemed to themselves to be people victorious and wise; their having hair like women's hair means that they seemed to themselves to have an affection for what is true; their teeth being like those of lions means that the power of the senses, which are the last and lowest on the natural level of a person, seemed to them to make them powerful over everything; their breastplates being like breastplates of iron means the kinds of arguments, based on ideas that are delusions, which they use to fight with and are strong in; the noise of their wings like the noise of chariots of many horses running into battle means reasonings seemingly formed from the truths of teaching drawn from the Word, truths they must fight to defend; their having tails which were like scorpions means notions that were convincing; their having the stings in their tails means abilities to deceive by means of those notions; their power to hurt people for five months means that they produce a kind of indifference in those with an understanding of what is true and a perception of what is good; their having over them a king, the angel of the abyss, whose name is Abaddon or Apollyon, means that their falsities came from hell, where those who are entirely natural and ruled by their own intelligence reside.

3

Such is the spiritual sense of these words, nothing of which is apparent in the literal sense. The same is so everywhere else in the Book of Revelation. It should be recognized that in the spiritual sense everything stands together in a continuous sequence which each expression in the literal or natural sense contributes towards. If therefore even a small part of an expression were removed the sequence would be interrupted and the link broken, and so to guard against this happening the end of this prophetical book adds that not a word should be taken away from it, Rev.22:19. The like applied to the books of Prophets belonging to the Old Testament, from which not a thing was to be taken away; in the Lord's Divine providence it happened that details in them, down to the actual letters, were numbered, and this was done by the Massoretes.

4

14   Where the Lord speaks in the presence of His disciples about the ending of the age, meaning the last stage of the church, He says

Statim post afflictionem dierum illorum sol obscurabitur, et luna non dabit lumen suum, et stellae cadent de caelo, et potentiae caelorum commovebuntur. Et tunc apparebit signum Filii Hominis in caelo, et tunc plangent omnes tribus terrae; et videbunt Filium Hominis venientem in nubibus caeli cum potentia et gloria multa. Et emittet angelos cum tubae voce magna, et congregabunt electos Ipsius a quatuor ventis ab extremo caelorum usque ad extremum illorum. Matt.24:29-31.

Per haec in sensu spirituali non intelligitur quod sol et luna obscurarentur, quod stellae caderent de caelo, quodque appariturum esset signum Domini in caelo, et quod visuri Ipsum in nubibus, et simul angelos cum tubis; sed per singula verba ibi intelliguntur spiritualia quae ecclesiae sunt, de cujus statu in fine illa dicta sunt. In sensu enim spirituali per solem, qui obscurabitur, intelligitur Dominus quoad amorem; per lunam, quae non dabit lumen suum, Dominus quoad fidem; per stellas quae cadent de caelo, cognitiones boni et veri quae periturae; per signum Filii Hominis in caelo, apparitio Divini Veri, per tribus terrae, quae plangent, defectus omnis veri quod fidei, et boni quod amoris; per adventum Filii Hominis in nubibus caeli cum potentia et gloria, praesentia Domini in Verbo et revelatio; per nubes significatur Verbi sensus literae et per gloriam Verbi sensus spiritualis; per angelos cum tubae voce magna significatur caelum unde Divinum Verum; per congregare electos a quatuor ventis ab extremo caelorum ad extremum illorum significatur novum ecclesiae quoad amorem et fidem.

Quod non intelligatur obscuratio solis et lunae, ac delapsus stellarum in terram, constat manifeste ex Prophetis, apud quos similia dicuntur de ecclesiae statu, quando Dominus in mundum venturus est. Ut apud Esaiam,

Ecce dies Jehovae venit, saevus, et excandescentiae et irae. Stellae caelorum, et sidera illorum, non lucebunt luce sua, obtenebrabitur sol in ortu suo, et luna non splendere faciet lumen suum. Visitabo super orbem malitiam. 13:9-11.

---

    6   cum tubae voce magna *VR*: cum tuba et voce magna *SS*
  23   ditto
  31   excandescentiae et irae: excandescentiae irae *SS, VR*

towards the end of the predictions of its consecutive changes of state, Immediately after the affliction of those days the sun will be darkened, and the moon will not give its light, and the stars will fall from the sky, and the powers of the heavens will be shaken. And then will the sign of the Son of Man appear in the sky, and then all the tribes of the earth will wail; and they will see the Son of Man coming in the clouds of heaven with power and great glory. And He will send forth angels with a loud blast of a trumpet, and they will gather His chosen from the four winds from one end of the heavens to the other. Matt.24:29-31.

In the spiritual sense this does not mean that the sun and the moon would be darkened, stars would fall from the sky, and the Lord's sign would appear in the sky, and that they would see Him in the clouds accompanied by angels with trumpets. Rather, all the expressions here have spiritual meanings referring to the church; and they describe its state at its end. For in the spiritual sense the sun, which will be darkened, means the Lord so far as love is concerned; the moon, which will not give its light, means the Lord so far as faith is concerned; the stars, which will fall from the sky, means items of knowledge concerning goodness and truth, which are going to be destroyed; the sign of the Son of Man in heaven means the manifestation of Divine Truth; the tribes of the earth, who will wail, means the lack of all truth to do with faith, and of goodness to do with love; the coming of the Son of Man in the clouds of heaven with power and glory means the Lord's presence and His revelation in the Word, clouds meaning the literal sense of the Word and glory the spiritual sense of the Word; the angels with a loud blast of the trumpet mean heaven from which Divine Truth comes; gathering the chosen from the four winds from one end of the heavens to the other means a new existence in the church of love and faith. 2

It is quite plain that the darkening of the sun and the moon is not meant, nor the falling of stars to earth, because of the Prophets, where similar statements are made about the state of the church at the time the Lord was to come into the world. For instance, in Isaiah, 3

Behold, the day of Jehovah is coming, cruel, and one of wrath and anger. The stars of the skies and their constellations will not shine with their light, the sun will be darkened in its rising, and the moon will not cause its light to shine. I shall visit upon the world its wickedness. 13:9-11.

Apud Joelem,

Venit dies Jehovae, dies tenebrarum et caliginis. Sol et luna atrati erunt, et stellae contrahent splendorem suum. 3:4; 4:15.

Apud Ezechielem,

Obtegam caelos, et atrabo stellas; solem nube obtegam, et luna non lucere faciet lumen suum. Omnia luminaria lucis obtenebrabo, et dabo tenebras super terra. 32:7,8.

Per diem Jehovae intelligitur adventus Domini, qui fuit quando non amplius erat aliquod bonum et verum in ecclesia residuum, et non aliqua cognitio Domini.
15   Ut videatur quod prophetica Verbi Veteris Testamenti in multis locis absque sensu spirituali non intelligantur, velim solum aliqua adducere. Ut hoc apud Esaiam,

Tunc excitabit Jehovah contra Aschurem flagellum, juxta plagam Midianis in petra Oreb; et baculus ejus super mari, quem tollet in via Aegypti. Et fiet in die, recedet onus ejus desuper humero tuo, et jugum desuper collo tuo. Veniet contra Ajath, transibit in Migronem, contra Michmasch mandabit armis suis. Transibunt Mabaram, Geba diversorium nobis, trepidabit Ramah, Gibea Schaulis fugiet. Ejula voce tua, filia Gallim; ausculta, Lajisch – misera Anathoth. Vagabitur Madmena; habitatores Gebim congregabunt se. Adhucne dies in Nob ad consistendum? movebit manum suam mons filiae Zionis, collis Hierosolymae. Jehovah excidet implexa sylvae ferro, et Libanus per Magnificum cadet. 10:26-34.

Hic sola nomina occurrunt, ex quibus nihil potest hauriri nisi ope sensus spiritualis, in quo omnia nomina in Verbo significant res caeli et ecclesiae. Ex illo sensu colligitur quod per illa significetur quod tota ecclesia per scientifica

3   3:4; 4:15 SS^1, SS^2, VR^1, VR^2: 2:1,2,10; 4:15 SS^3, VR^3
18   Michmasch SS^3: Mischmath SS^1, SS^2
18   Mabaram: Mebaram SS
19   Geba: Gibea SS
24   26-34: 24-34 SS

In Joel,

The day of Jehovah is coming, a day of gloominess and thick darkness. The sun and the moon will be turned black, and the stars will withdraw their shining. 2:31[1]; 3:15.

In Ezekiel,

I shall cover the heavens and make the stars black; I shall cover the sun with a cloud, and the moon will not cause its light to shine. I shall darken all the luminaries and bring darkness upon the earth. 32:7,8.

The day of Jehovah means the Lord's coming, which took place when there was no more goodness and truth left in the church, nor any knowledge of the Lord.

15   To let it be seen that the prophetical parts of the Old Testament Word are in many places unintelligible without the spiritual sense I would just like to quote some of them. For instance, in Isaiah,

At that time Jehovah will arouse the scourge against Asshur, as when Midian was smitten at the rock of Oreb, and his rod will be over the sea, which he will lift up in the way of Egypt. And it will happen on that day, that his burden will depart from upon your shoulder, and his yoke from upon your neck. He will come against Aiath, pass over against Migron, order his weapons against Michmash. They will pass over the Mebarah, Geba will be a lodging place for us, Ramah will tremble, Gibeah of Saul will flee. Wail with your voice, O daughter of Gallim; listen, O Laish – poor Anathoth. Madmenah will wander about; the inhabitants of Gebim will gather themselves together. This day is he not in Nob to stay; the mountain of the daughter of Zion, the hill of Jerusalem, will shake her fist. Jehovah will cut down the entangled boughs of the wood with an axe, and Lebanon will fall by a Majestic One. 10:26-34.

Here mere names are used from which nothing can be gleaned without the help of the spiritual sense, in which all the names appearing in the Word mean the realities of heaven and the church. The meaning of all this may be gathered from that sense, which is that the whole of the church was destroyed by factual knowledge

---

1   The editor of the third Latin edition of *SS* emended the chapter-and-verse numbering here from 3:4 to 2:1,2,10, but in the judgment of the present editor and his consultant 3:4 (2:31 in English versions of Joel) is indeed what Swedenborg intended

pervertentia omne verum et confirmantia falsum devastata sit. Alibi apud eundem Prophetam,

In die illo recedet aemulatio Ephraimi, et hostes Jehudae exscindentur; Ephraim non aemulabitur cum Jehuda, et Jehudah non angustabit
5 Ephraimum. Sed involabunt in humerum Philisthaeorum versus mare, una depraedabuntur filios orientis; Edomus et Moabus emissio manus eorum. Contra devovebit Jehovah linguam maris Aegypti, et agitabit manum Suam super Fluvium cum vehementia spiritus Sui, et percutiet eum in septem rivos, ut viam faciat cum
10 calceis. Tunc erit semita reliquiis populi Ejus, quae residuae erunt ab Aschure. 11:13-16.

Hic quoque nemo, nisi qui scit quid per singula nomina ibi significatur, visurus est aliquod Divinum, cum tamen agitur ibi de Adventu Domini et quid tunc fiet, ut manifeste patet
15 a versu 1 ad 10 ibi. Quis itaque absque ope sensus spiritualis visurus est quod per illa in suo ordine significetur hoc, quod illi qui in falsis ex ignorantia sunt, et se non a malis seduci passi sunt, ad Dominum accessuri sint, et quod ecclesia tunc intellectura sit Verbum, et quod falsa tunc illis non amplius
20 nocitura sint?

Similiter ubi non sunt nomina, ut apud Ezechielem,

Sic dixit Dominus Jehovih, Fili hominis, dic avi omnis alae, et omni ferae agri, Congregamini et venite, congregate vos a circuitu ad sacrificium Meum quod sacrifico vobis, sacrificium magnum
25 super montibus Israelis, ut comedatis carnem et bibatis sanguinem. Carnem fortium comedetis et sanguinem principum terrae bibetis. Comedetis adipem ad satietatem, et bibetis sanguinem usque ad ebrietatem, de sacrificio Meo quod sacrifico vobis. Satiabimini super mensa Mea, equo et curru, et forti, et omni viro belli. Sic dabo
30 gloriam Meam inter gentes. 39:17-21.

Qui non ex sensu spirituali scit quid significat sacrificium, quid caro et sanguis, quidque equus, currus, fortis, et vir belli, non sciturus est aliud quam quod comesturi et bibituri sint talia. Sed sensus spiritualis docet quod per comedere carnem

used to distort everything true and justify what is false. In another place in the same prophet,

On that day the rivalry of Ephraim will depart, and the enemies of Judah will be cut off; Ephraim will not strive with Judah, and Judah will not harass Ephraim. But they will fly down onto the shoulder of the Philistines towards the sea, and together plunder the sons of the east; Edom and Moab will be the outstretching of their hand. Jehovah will utterly destroy the tongue of the sea of Egypt, and will wave His hand over the River with the might of His spirit, and strike it in the seven streams, to make it a way to go with shoes. Then there will be a highway for the remnant of His people which will remain from Asshur. 11:13-16.

Here also, no one unless they know the meanings of each of the names that are used will see anything Divine, when yet the subject here is the Lord's coming and what will happen then, as is perfectly clear from verses 1-10 of that chapter. Without the aid of the spiritual sense therefore is anyone going to see that by these names, in the order in which they occur, is meant this – that those who have false ideas owing to ignorance but do not allow themselves to be led astray by evil ways will come to the Lord, that the church will then have an understanding of the Word, and that false ideas will not then do them any harm?

Much the same may be said about verses in which no names are mentioned, such as these, in Ezekiel,

Thus said the Lord Jehovih, Son of man, say to every bird of the air and to every wild animal of the field, Gather together and come; gather yourselves together from all around to My sacrifice which I am sacrificing for you, a great sacrifice upon the mountains of Israel, so that you may eat flesh and drink blood. You will eat the flesh of the mighty and drink the blood of the princes of the earth. You will eat fat till you are glutted, and drink blood till you are drunk, from My sacrifice which I am sacrificing for you. You will be glutted at My table with horse and chariot, and the mighty one, and every man of war. Thus will I set My glory among the nations. 39:17-21.

Those who do not know from the spiritual sense what sacrifice means, what flesh and blood mean, and what horse, chariot, mighty one, and man of war mean, are not going to know anything other than that they are to eat and drink such things. But the spiritual sense shows that eating the flesh and drinking the blood from the sacrifice

et bibere sanguinem de sacrificio quod Dominus Jehovih super montibus Israelis dabit, significetur appropriare sibi Divinum bonum et Divinum verum ex Verbo; agitur enim ibi de convocatione omnium ad regnum Domini, et in specie de instauratione ecclesiae apud gentes a Domino. Quis non videre potest quod non caro per carnem nec sanguis per sanguinem ibi intelligatur, ut quod sanguinem biberent usque ad ebrietatem, et quod satiarentur equo, curru, forti, et omni viro belli? Similiter in mille aliis locis apud Prophetas.

16 Absque sensu spirituali non aliquis sciret, quare mandatum est Jeremiae Prophetae, ut emeret sibi cingulum, et poneret super lumbis, non traduceret illud per aquas, et absconderet in foramine petrae juxta Euphratem, Jer.13:1-7; quod mandatum sit Esaiae Prophetae, quod dissolveret saccum desuper lumbis, et calceum exueret desuper pede suo, ac iret nudus et discalceatus tres annos, Esai.20:2,3; quod mandatum sit Ezechieli Prophetae, quod novaculam traduceret super caput suum et super barbam suam, et postea divideret illa, tertiam partem combureret in medio urbis, tertiam percuteret gladio, tertiam dispergeret in ventum, et parum ex illis alligaret in alis, tandem projiceret in medium ignis, Ezech.5:1-4; quod eidem Prophetae mandatum sit, quod cubaret super latere suo sinistro et dextro 390 dies et 40 dies, et faceret sibi placentam ex triticis, hordeis, miliis, et zeis, cum excrementis bovis, et comederet illam, ac interea poneret vallum et aggerem contra Hierosolymam, et obsideret illam, Ezech.4:1-15; quod Hoscheae Prophetae bis mandatum sit, ut acciperet sibi meretricem in uxorem, Hos.1:2-9; 3:2,3; et plura similia.

Praeterea quis absque sensu spirituali sciret quid significatur per omnia tabernaculi, ut per arcam, propitiatorium, cherubos, candelabrum, altare suffitus, panes facierum super mensa, perque vela et aulaea ejus? Quis absque sensu spirituali sciret quid significatur per vestes sanctitatis Aharonis, ejus tunicam, pallium, ephodum, urim et thummim, cidarim, et plura ejus? Quis absque sensu spirituali sciret quid significatur per omnia illa quae mandata sunt de holocaustis, sacrificiis, minchis et libaminibus? tum de sabbathis et festis? Veritas est quod non minimum de illis fuerit mandatum quod non aliquid Domini, caeli et ecclesiae significaverit. Ex his paucis evidenter videri potest quod sensus spiritualis sit in omnibus et singulis Verbi.

23 sinistro et dextro SS^3: dextro et sinistro SS^1, SS^2

that the Lord Jehovih will make on the mountains of Israel mean taking into oneself Divine goodness and Divine truth obtained from the Word; for the subject at this point is the call to everyone to the Lord's kingdom, and in particular the establishment by the Lord of the church among the gentiles. Is there anyone who cannot see that flesh is not meant by flesh here, or blood by blood, as when it says that they were to drink blood till they were drunk and to be glutted with horse, chariot, mighty one, and every man of war? The like of this occurs in a thousand other places among the Prophets.

16   Without the spiritual sense no one would know why Jeremiah the prophet was commanded to buy a belt for himself and put it round his waist, not to take it through water but to hide it in a cleft of a rock beside the Euphrates, Jer.13:1-7; why Isaiah the prophet was commanded to loose the sackcloth from round his waist and to remove the shoes from over his feet, and to go naked and barefoot for three years, Isa.20:2,3; why Ezekiel the prophet was commanded to pass a razor over his head and beard, and then divide the shaven-off hairs, burning a third in the middle of the city, striking a third with a sword, scattering a third to the wind, and binding a small part of them in the skirts of his robe, finally casting them into the midst of the fire, Ezek.5:1-4; why the same prophet was commanded to lie on his left side and on his right, for 390 days and 40 days, to make a cake for himself of wheat, barley, millet, and spelt, mixed with ox dung, and to eat it, and in the meantime to set up a rampart and mound against Jerusalem and lay siege against it, Ezek.4:1-15; why Hosea the prophet was twice commanded to take to himself a prostitute as his wife, Hos.1:2-9; 3:2,3; and more like all this.

Furthermore without the spiritual sense would anyone know what is meant by all that comprises the tabernacle, such as the ark, mercy seat, cherubs, lampstand, altar of burnt incense, loaves of the presence on the table, and its veils and curtains? Without the spiritual sense would anyone know what is meant by Aaron's holy garments – his tunic, robe, ephod, urim and thummim, turban, and more? Without the spiritual sense who would know what is meant by all that was commanded concerning burnt offerings, sacrifices, meal offerings and drink offerings? Also about sabbaths and festivals? The truth is that not the least of those things was commanded that did not mean something to do with the Lord, heaven and the church. These few examples enable it to be seen clearly that the spiritual sense is present in every single detail of the Word.

17   Quod Dominus cum in mundo fuit loquutus sit per correspondentias, ita spiritualiter cum naturaliter, constare potest ex parabolis Ipsius, in quarum singulis vocibus inest sensus spiritualis. Exemplo sit parabola de decem virginibus; dixit,

Simile est regnum caelorum decem virginibus, quae accipientes lampadas suas exiverunt in occursum Sponsi. Quinque ex illis erant prudentes, quinque vero stultae. Quae erant stultae, accipientes lampadas suas non acceperunt oleum; prudentes vero acceperunt oleum in lampadibus suis. Tardante vero Sponso dormitarunt omnes et obdormierunt. Media autem nocte clamor factus est, Ecce Sponsus venit; exite in occursum Ejus. Tunc expergefactae omnes virgines istae, et adornarunt lampadas suas. Verum stultae prudentibus dixerunt, Date nobis de oleo vestro, quia lampades nostrae exstinguuntur. Verum responderunt prudentes, dicentes, Ne forte non sufficiat nobis et vobis; abite potius ad vendentes et emite vobis ipsis. At abeuntibus illis ad emendum, venit Sponsus, et paratae ingressae sunt cum Ipso ad nuptias, et ostium clausum est. Et tandem veniunt etiam reliquae virgines, dicentes, Domine, Domine, aperi nobis. Ille vero respondens dixit, Amen dico vobis, non novi vos. Matt.25:1-12.

Quod in singulis his sit sensus spiritualis, et inde sanctum Divinum, non videt nisi qui scit quod sensus spiritualis sit, et qualis ille. In sensu spirituali per regnum caelorum intelligitur caelum et ecclesia, per Sponsum Dominus, per nuptias conjugium Domini cum caelo et ecclesia per bonum amoris et fidei. Per virgines significantur illi qui ab ecclesia sunt, per decem omnes, per quinque aliquae, per lampadas vera fidei, per oleum bonum amoris; per dormire et expergisci vita hominis in mundo, quae naturalis, et vita ejus post mortem, quae spiritualis; per emere, comparare sibi; per ire ad vendentes et emere oleum, comparare sibi bonum amoris ab aliis post mortem; et quia tunc non amplius comparatur, ideo tametsi cum lampadibus et empto oleo ad ostium, ubi nuptiae erant, venerunt, usque illis dictum est a Sponso, Non novi vos; causa est quia homo post vitam in mundo manet qualis in mundo vixerat.

    6   lampadas *SS*¹, *SS*³: lampades *SS*², *VR*
    8   ditto
    12   ditto
    23   caelorum *VR*: Dei *SS*
    27   lampadas: lampades *SS*, *VR*

17   The Lord when He was in the world spoke by means of correspondences, so He spoke spiritually as well as naturally. This becomes clear from His parables, the individual expressions of which contain a spiritual sense. Take for example the parable of the ten virgins. He said,

The kingdom of the heavens is like ten virgins, who took their lamps and went out to meet the Bridegroom. Five of them were wise, but five were foolish. The foolish ones, when they took their lamps, failed to take oil; but the wise ones took oil in their lamps. But when the Bridegroom was late, they all became drowsy and went off to sleep. However, in the middle of the night a cry went up, Behold, the Bridegroom is coming; go out to meet Him. Then all these virgins woke up and trimmed their lamps. But the foolish ones said to the wise ones, Give us some of your oil, for our lamps are going out. But the wise ones replied and said, Perhaps there may not be enough for us and for you; go rather to the sellers and buy some for yourselves. While they were away buying the Bridegroom came, and those who were ready went in with Him to the wedding; and the door was shut. At length the other virgins came too and said, Lord, Lord, open the door to us. But He replied and said, In truth I tell you, I do not know you. Matt.25:1-12.

2   No one who does not know that there is a spiritual sense, and what sort of sense it is, can see that each of these details contains a spiritual sense, and therefore a Divine holiness. In the spiritual sense the kingdom of the heavens means heaven and the church, the Bridegroom means the Lord, the wedding the Lord's marriage with heaven and the church by means of the goodness of love and faith. The virgins mean those who belong to the church, ten means all, five some, lamps the truths of faith, oil the goodness of love. Sleeping and waking up mean people's life in the world, which is natural, and their life after death, which is spiritual. Buying means acquiring, going to the sellers and buying oil means acquiring the goodness of love from others after death. Because it cannot then any longer be acquired, although they came with their lamps and the oil they had bought to the door where the wedding was, still the Bridegroom told them, I do not know you. This is because after their life in the world people remain such as their life in the world has made them.

Ex his patet quod Dominus per meras correspondentias loquutus sit, et hoc quia ex Divino, quod in Ipso et Ipsius erat. Quod Sponsus significet Dominum, et regnum caelorum ecclesiam, et quod nuptiae significent conjugium Domini cum ecclesia per bonum amoris et fidei, virgines illos qui ab ecclesia, decem omnes, quinque aliquos, dormire statum naturalem, emere comparare sibi, ostium ingressum ad caelum, ac non nosse, cum a Domino, non esse in amore Ipsius, constare potest a multis locis in Verbo Prophetico, ubi illa significant similia. Quia virgines significant illos qui ab ecclesia sunt, ideo toties in Verbo Prophetico dicitur virgo et filia Zionis, Hierosolymae, Israelis; et quia oleum significat bonum amoris, ideo omnia sancta Ecclesiae Israeliticae oleo ungebantur. Simile est in reliquis parabolis, et in omnibus verbis quae Dominus loquutus est, et apud Evangelistas scripta sunt. Inde est quod Dominus dicat quod verba Ipsius spiritus et vita sint, Joh.6:63.

Simile est cum omnibus Domini miraculis, quae Divina erant, quia varios status, apud quos ecclesia a Domino instauranda erat, significaverunt, ut quod caeci receperint visum significavit quod illi intelligentiam, qui in ignorantia veri fuerunt, acciperent; quod surdi receperint auditum significavit quod illi auscultarent et obedirent qui nihil prius de Domino et de Verbo audiverunt; quod mortui resuscitati sint significavit quod vivi fierent qui alioquin spiritualiter perirent; et sic porro. Hoc intelligitur per Domini responsum ad discipulos Johannis, interrogantis num Ille esset qui venturus,

Annuntiate Johanni quae auditis et videtis: caeci vident et claudi ambulant, leprosi mundantur et surdi audiunt, mortui resurgunt et pauperes audiunt Evangelium. Matt.11:3-5.

Praeterea omnia miracula in Verbo memorata, in se continent talia quae Domini, caeli et ecclesiae sunt; per id sunt illa miracula Divina et distinguuntur a miraculis non Divinis. Haec pauca sint illustrationi quid sensus spiritualis, et quod ille sit in omnibus et singulis Verbi.

18 iii **Quod ex sensu spirituali sit quod Verbum sit divinitus inspiratum, ac in omni voce sanctum.** Dicitur in ecclesia

12 Hierosolymae, SS: Hierosolymae, Jehudae, VR
37 ac VR: et SS

From all this it is plain that the Lord spoke purely in 3
correspondences, and this was because He spoke from the Divine
which was in Him and was His. As for the Bridegroom meaning
the Lord, the kingdom of the heavens the church, and the wedding
the Lord's marriage with the church by means of the goodness of
love and faith; the virgins meaning those who belong to the church,
ten all, five some; while sleeping means a natural state, buying
acquiring, the door the entrance to heaven, and not knowing, when
said by the Lord, meaning not abiding in His love, all this becomes
clear from many places in the prophetic parts of the Word in which
these words or phrases have similar meanings. It is because virgins
mean those who belong to the church that so often in the prophetic
parts of the Word the expressions virgin and daughter of Zion, of
Jerusalem, and of Israel occur, and it was because oil means the
goodness of love that all the holy things of the Israelite Church were
anointed with oil. It is the same in the rest of the parables and in all
the expressions used by the Lord and written in the Gospels. This is
why the Lord says, His words are spirit and life, John 6:63.

The same applies to all the Lord's miracles. They were 4
Divine, because they were signs of the different states of people with
whom the church was to be established by the Lord, for instance, the
blind receiving their sight was a sign that those unacquainted with
the truth would receive understanding; the deaf receiving hearing
was a sign that those who had previously heard nothing about the
Lord or the Word would listen and obey; the dead being raised was
a sign that those who would have otherwise perished spiritually
would be made alive; and so on. This is what should be understood
by the Lord's reply to John's disciples who asked Him whether He
was the one who was to come,

Tell John the things which you hear and see: the blind see, and the lame
walk, lepers are cleansed and the deaf hear, the dead rise again and the
poor hear the gospel. Matt.11:3-5.

Furthermore all the miracles mentioned in the Word contain within
them the kinds of things that relate to the Lord, heaven and the
church, and for that reason those miracles are Divine and different
from those which are not Divine. The few that have been spoken
of here serve to show what the spiritual sense is, and that this is
present in every single detail of the Word.

18   iii **It is the spiritual sense which makes the Word divinely inspired and holy in every word.** People in the church say that

quod Verbum sit sanctum, et hoc quia Jehovah Deus illud loquutus est. Sed quia sanctum ejus ex sola litera non apparet, ideo qui propterea de sanctitate ejus semel dubitat, deinde ille cum legit Verbum, se per multa ibi confirmat. Cogitat enim tunc, Num hoc sanctum? Num hoc Divinum? Ne itaque talis cogitatio apud multos influat et postea invalescat, et per id conjunctio Domini cum ecclesia, in qua est Verbum, pereat, placuit Domino nunc sensum spiritualem revelare, ut sciatur ubinam illud sanctum in Verbo latet. Sed exempla hoc quoque illustrent.

In Verbo nunc agitur de Aegypto, nunc de Aschure, nunc de Edomo, de Moabo, de filiis Ammonis, de Tyro et Zidone, de Gogo. Qui non scit quod per nomina illorum significentur res caeli et ecclesiae, in errorem abduci potest quod Verbum multum de gentibus et populis agat, et modo parum de caelo et ecclesia, ita multum de terrestribus et parum de caelestibus. Sed cum ille scit quid per illos seu per nomina illorum significatur, ab errore in veritatem potest venire.

Similiter dum in Verbo videt quod ibi toties nominentur horti, luci, sylvae, tum arbores illorum, ut olea, vitis, cedrus, populus, quercus, ut et quod toties agnus, ovis, hircus, vitulus, bos, et quoque montes, colles, valles, et ibi fontes, fluvii, aquae, et plura similia. Ille qui nihil scit de sensu spirituali Verbi non potest aliter credere quam quod solum illa sint quae intelliguntur; non scit enim quod per hortum, lucum, et sylvam intelligantur sapientia, intelligentia, et scientia; quod per oleam, vitem, cedrum, populum, et quercum intelligantur ecclesiae bonum et verum caeleste, spirituale, rationale, naturale, et sensuale; quod per agnum, ovem, hircum, vitulum, bovem intelligantur innocentia, charitas, et affectio naturalis; quod per montes, colles, et valles intelligantur superiora, inferiora, et infima ecclesiae; tum quod per Aegyptum significetur scientia, per Aschurem ratio, per Edomum naturale, per Moabum adulteratio boni, per filios Ammonis adulteratio veri, per Tyrum et Zidonem cognitiones veri et boni, per Gogum cultus externus absque interno. Cum autem haec scit, tunc potest cogitare quod Verbum non agat nisi quam de caelestibus, et quod terrestria illa modo sint subjecta in quibus illa sunt.

1   et *VR*: at *SS*
4   se per multa ibi confirmat *VR*: se per multa ibi se confirmat *SS¹*; per multa ibi se confirmat *SS²*, *SS³*

the Word is holy, and that this is because Jehovah God spoke it. But because its holiness is not apparent in the literal sense alone, once any, on account of that, begin to doubt its holiness, they soon find much to warrant such doubt when they read the Word; for they think, This surely cannot be holy? Surely this is not Divine? Therefore to prevent this way of thinking from affecting a large number of people and then becoming prevalent, as a result of which the link between the Lord and the church, where the Word is, would be broken, it is the Lord's good pleasure now to reveal the spiritual sense, so that it may be known where that holiness hidden in the Word lies. Let some examples also be given to illustrate this.

At various places in the Word there is talk of Egypt, Assyria, Edom, Moab, the children of Ammon, Tyre and Sidon, and Gog. People who do not know that these names stand for matters relating to heaven and the church may be led into the erroneous belief that the Word has much to say about nations and peoples, and only a little about heaven and the church, much, that is, on earthly subjects and little on heavenly ones. But when they know what is meant by those peoples or their names they can progress from their erroneous belief to a true one.

It is similar when they see in the Word so many mentions of a garden, a grove, a wood, or the trees in them, such as the olive, the vine, the cedar, the poplar, or the oak; or so many mentions of the lamb, the sheep, the goat, the calf, or the ox; or of mountains, hills, valleys and the springs, rivers, and waters in them, or many other similar things. People who know nothing of the spiritual sense of the Word cannot help thinking that it is merely these things which are intended. For they are unaware that garden, grove, and wood mean wisdom, intelligence, and knowledge, or that olive, vine, cedar, poplar, and oak mean the goodness and truth of the church in their celestial, spiritual, rational, natural, and sensory forms. Nor do they know that lamb, sheep, goat, calf, and ox mean innocence, charity, and natural affection; or that mountains, hills, and valleys mean the highest, lower, and lowest elements in the church. Nor do they know that Egypt means knowledge, Assyria reason, Edom the natural level, Moab the adulteration of goodness, the children of Ammon the adulteration of truth, Tyre and Sidon the knowledge of truth and goodness, Gog external worship without any internal. But once they do know these meanings it is possible for them to reflect that the Word speaks only of heavenly matters, and those earthly matters are merely the underlying supports of the others.

Sed exemplum ex Verbo hoc etiam illustret. Legitur apud Davidem,

Vox Jehovae super aquis, Deus gloriae tonare facit, Jehovah super aquis magnis. Vox Jehovae frangens cedros, confringit Jehovah cedros Libani, et saltare facit eos sicut vitulum, Libanum et Schirjonem sicut filium monocerotum, vox Jehovae incidens ut flamma ignis. Vox Jehovae trepidare facit desertum; trepidare facit desertum Kadesh. Vox Jehovae parturire facit cervas, et denudat sylvas. Sed in templo Ipsius quivis dicit Gloriam. Ps.29:3-9.

Qui non scit quod singula ibi quoad unamquamvis vocem Sancta Divina sint, ille potest, si mere naturalis est, secum dicere, Quid hoc, quod Jehovah sedeat super aquis, quod per vocem Suam frangat cedros, saltare faciat illos sicut vitulum, et Libanum sicut filium monocerotum, quod parturire faciat cervas, et plura? Nescit enim quod potentia Divini Veri seu Verbi per illa in sensu spirituali descripta sit. Nam in illo sensu, per vocem Jehovae, quae ibi est tonitru, intelligitur Divinum Verum seu Verbum in sua potentia; per aquas magnas, super quibus Jehovah sedet, intelliguntur vera ejus; per cedros et per Libanum, quos frangit et confringit, intelliguntur falsa rationalis hominis; per vitulum et filium monocerotum, falsa naturalis et sensualis hominis; per flammam ignis, affectio falsi; per desertum et desertum Kadesh, ecclesia ubi non aliquod verum et bonum; per cervas, quas vox Jehovae parturire facit, intelliguntur gentes quae in bono naturali sunt, et per sylvas, quas denudat, intelliguntur scientiae et cognitiones, quas Verbum illis aperit. Quare sequitur, In templo Ipsius quivis dicit Gloriam, per quod intelligitur quod in singulis Verbi sint Divina vera; templum enim significat Dominum, et inde Verbum, tum caelum et ecclesiam, et gloria significat Divinum Verum. Ex his patet quod nulla vox ibi sit quae non Divinam potentiam Verbi contra falsa omnis generis apud naturales homines, ac Divinam potentiam reformandi gentes, describit.

19   Est sensus adhuc interior in Verbo, qui **caelestis** vocatur, de quo aliquid supra, n.6, dictum est. Sed hic sensus aegre potest enodari, non enim ita cadit in cogitationem intellectus

Let an example be given from the Word to illustrate this 4
point also. It says in David,

The voice of Jehovah is upon the waters, the God of glory causes it to thunder, Jehovah is upon great waters. The voice of Jehovah breaking cedars, Jehovah breaks to pieces the cedars of Lebanon, and makes them skip like a calf, Lebanon and Sirion like the offspring of a unicorn, the voice of Jehovah striking like a flame of fire. The voice of Jehovah causes the wilderness to shake, it causes the wilderness of Kadesh to shake. The voice of Jehovah causes the hinds to give birth, and strips the forests bare. But in His temple everyone says, Glory! Ps.29:3-9.

People who do not know that each word of everything stated here is holy and Divine cannot help saying to themselves if they are thinking on a merely natural level, What does this mean, that Jehovah sits upon waters, that by means of His voice He breaks cedars, causing them to skip like a calf, and Lebanon like the offspring of a unicorn, that He causes hinds to give birth, and so on? This is because they do not know that these things in the spiritual sense describe the power of Divine Truth, that is, of the Word. For in that sense *voice of Jehovah*, which in this instance is thunder, stands for the power Divine Truth or the Word possesses; *great waters* which Jehovah sits upon stand for its truths; *cedars* and *Lebanon*, which He breaks and breaks to pieces, stand for false ideas belonging to the rational level of human thinking; *calf* and the *offspring of a unicorn* stand for false ideas belonging to the natural and sensory level of it; *flame of fire* stands for love of what is false; *wilderness* and *wilderness of Kadesh* stand for a church where there is not anything true or good; *hinds* which the voice of Jehovah causes to give birth stand for nations possessing natural goodness, and *forests* which it strips bare for knowledge and concepts which the Word gives them. This being so the Psalm goes on to say, *In His temple everyone says, Glory!* meaning that Divine truths are contained in every detail of the Word; for *temple* means the Lord, and consequently the Word, as well as heaven and the church, and *glory* means Divine Truth. From this it is evident that not one expression appears there which does not serve to describe the Divine power of the Word opposed to every kind of false idea existing with natural-minded people, or to describe the Divine power to transform gentiles.

19   There is in the Word a sense still more internal, termed **the celestial**, about which something was said above, in §6. But it is barely possible to draw this sense out because it has a place not

sicut in affectionem voluntatis. Quod interior adhuc sensus, qui caelestis vocatur, insit Verbo, est quia a Domino procedit Divinum Bonum et Divinum Verum – Divinum Bonum ex Divino Amore Ipsius, et Divinum Verum ex Divina Sapientia Ipsius. Utrumque est in Verbo, nam Verbum est Divinum Procedens; et quia utrumque est, ideo Verbum vivificat illos qui id sancte legunt. Sed de hac re dicetur in articulo ubi demonstrabitur quod in singulis Verbi sit conjugium Domini et ecclesiae, et inde conjugium boni et veri.

20   iv **Quod sensus spiritualis Verbi hactenus ignotus fuerit.** Quod omnia et singula quae in natura sunt correspondeant spiritualibus, similiter omnia et singula quae in corpore humano, ostensum est in opere **De Caelo et Inferno** n.87-115. Sed quid correspondentia, hactenus nescitum est; verum in antiquissimis temporibus, notissima fuit, illis enim qui tunc vixerunt fuit scientia correspondentiarum scientia scientiarum, et tam universalis ut omnes illorum codices et libri per correspondentias scripti sint. Liber Hiobi, qui est liber antiquus, correspondentiis plenus est.

Hieroglyphica Aegyptiorum, et quoque fabulosa vetustissimorum, non alia fuerunt. Omnes ecclesiae antiquae fuerunt ecclesiae repraesentativae caelestium; ritus illarum, et quoque statuta, secundum quae institutus fuit cultus illarum, constabant ex meris correspondentiis. Similiter omnia ecclesiae apud filios Jacobi. Holocausta et sacrificia, cum singulis illorum, correspondentiae fuerunt, similiter tabernaculum cum omnibus inibi; tum etiam festa illorum, ut festum azymorum, festum tabernaculorum, et festum primitiarum; etiam sacerdotium Aharonis et Levitarum, ut et vestes sanctitatis Aharonis et filiorum ejus; et praeterea omnia statuta et judicia, quae cultum et vitam illorum concernebant. Et quia Divina in mundo se sistunt per correspondentias, ideo Verbum per meras correspondentias scriptum est, quare Dominus, quia loquutus est ex Divino Suo, loquutus est per correspondentias, nam quod a Divino est, hoc in natura cadit in talia quae Divinis correspondent, et quae tunc Divina, quae vocantur caelestia et spiritualia, in sinu suo recondunt.

21   Instructus sum quod homines Antiquissimae Ecclesiae, quae fuit ante Diluvium, tam caelesti genio fuerint ut

---

14   115: 105 *SS, VR*

so much in thought belonging to the understanding as in affection belonging to the will or intent. The reason why a sense still more internal, termed the celestial, is present within the Word is that from the Lord come forth Divine Goodness and Divine Truth – Divine Goodness from His Divine Love, and Divine Truth from His Divine Wisdom. Both of these exist in the Word, for the Word is a Divine Coming Forth; and because both exist there the Word gives life to those who read it with reverence. But this subject will be discussed in the section where it will be shown that in every detail of the Word there is a marriage of the Lord and the church, and therefore a marriage of goodness and truth.

20   iv **The spiritual sense of the Word has up to the present been unknown.** Every single thing to be found in nature corresponds to something spiritual, and likewise every single part of the human body, as was shown in the work **Heaven and Hell**, §§87-115. But up to the present it has remained unknown what correspondence is. Yet in the most ancient times it was very well known, for those who lived at that period regarded the knowledge of correspondences as the outstanding science, and it was so universally known that all their documents and books were written by means of correspondences. The Book of Job, which is an ancient book, is full of correspondences.

The hieroglyphic writings of the Egyptians, as well as the myths of the oldest peoples, were nothing else. All the ancient churches served to represent heavenly ideas; their rites and the rules which governed the establishment of their modes of worship were made up of nothing but correspondences. The same is true of all the details of the church among the children of Jacob. Their burnt offerings and sacrifices, and all that went with these, had meaning as correspondences, likewise the tabernacle and all its contents, as well as their festivals, such as the feast of unleavened bread, the feast of tabernacles, and the feast of first fruits, and also the priesthood of Aaron and the Levites, together with the holy vestments of Aaron and his sons, and in addition all the laws and judgments governing their worship and way of life. And since Divine ideas are presented in the world through correspondences, this and no other is the way the Word was written. Therefore the Lord, since He spoke from His Divine, spoke in correspondences. For whatever is Divine descends at the natural level into the kinds of things which correspond to Divine ones, and then contain in their inmost the Divine things called celestial and spiritual.

21   I have been informed that the people of the Most Ancient church, which existed before the Flood, had such heavenly

loquuti sint cum angelis caeli, et quod loqui potuerint cum illis per correspondentias. Inde status sapientiae illorum factus est talis ut quicquid viderent in tellure, non modo cogitarent de illo naturaliter sed etiam simul, spiritualiter, ita quoque conjunctim cum angelis. Insuper instructus sum quod Chanoch – de quo memoratur in Gen.5:21-24 – cum consociis suis, ex ore illorum collegerit correspondentias, ac scientiam illarum propagaverit ad posteros, ex quo factum est quod scientia correspondentiarum in multis regnis Asiae non modo nota fuerit sed etiam exculta, imprimis in terra Canaane, Aegypto, Assyria, Chaldaea, Syria, Arabia, in Tyro, Zidone, Ninive, et quod inde e locis maritimis translata sit in Graeciam, sed ibi versa in fabulosa, ut constare potest ex vetustissimorum scriptis ibi.

22   Sed cum repraesentativa ecclesiae, quae erant correspondentiae, temporis tractu versa sunt in idololatrica, et quoque in magica, tunc illa scientia ex Divina Domini providentia successive obliterata est, et apud gentem Israeliticam et Judaicam prorsus deperdita et exstincta. Cultus quidem hujus gentis constabat ex meris correspondentiis, et inde erat ille repraesentativus caelestium; sed usque illi nesciebant quid aliquod significabat, erant enim prorsus naturales homines, et inde non scire volebant nec poterant aliquid de spiritualibus, proinde nec aliquid de correspondentiis.

23   Quod idololatriae gentium antiquis temporibus ex scientia correspondentiarum traxerint originem, erat ex causa quia omnia quae apparent super tellure, correspondent, ita non modo arbores sed etiam pecudes et aves omnis generis, tum pisces et reliqua. Antiqui, qui in scientia correspondentiarum fuerunt, fecerunt sibi imagines quae caelestibus correspondebant, et illis delectabantur quia significabant talia quae caeli et inde ecclesiae erant, et ideo illa non modo in suis templis sed etiam in suis domibus posuerunt, non adorationis causa sed recordationis rei caelestis quam significabant. Inde in Aegypto et alibi fuerunt in imagine vituli, boves, serpentes, tum pueri, senes, virgines, quia vituli et boves significabant affectiones et vires naturalis hominis, serpentes prudentiam sensualis hominis, pueri innocentiam et charitatem, senes sapientiam, et virgines affectiones veri, et sic porro. Posteri, quando scientia correspondentiarum obliterata est, caeperunt

characters that they conversed with angels in heaven. They were able to do this by correspondences. So they reached such a pitch of wisdom that they not only thought naturally about anything they saw on earth, but at the same time also thought spiritually about it, and this established their link with angels. I have also been informed that Enoch, who is mentioned in Gen.5:21-24, together with his colleagues collected these correspondences by listening to their talk, and transmitted this science to posterity. As a result the science of correspondences was not merely known but also held in high esteem in many Asiatic kingdoms, especially in the land of Canaan, Egypt, Assyria, Chaldaea, Syria, Arabia, and in Tyre, Sidon, and Nineveh. And from there, from the coastal regions, it was transmitted to Greece, but was there transformed into myths, as is evident in the earliest Greek authors.

22   But when representative forms within the church, which were correspondences, were turned in the course of time into idolatrous practices, and even magical ones, the Lord's Divine providence ensured that the science should be gradually wiped out, and among the Israelite and Jewish nation totally lost and non-existent. This nation's worship consisted purely of correspondences, and was therefore representative of heavenly things, but still they were unaware what any detail meant. For they were purely natural people, so they neither wished nor were able to have any knowledge of spiritual things, or anything consequently of correspondences.

23   The reason why the idolatrous practices of nations in antiquity originated from the science of correspondences was that everything to be seen on earth has a corresponding meaning; this is true not only of trees but also animals and birds of every kind, as well as fish and other things. The ancient people who possessed the science of correspondences made themselves images to correspond to heavenly ideas, and they took pleasure in them because they stood for such things as concern heaven and consequently the church. They placed these images therefore not only in their temples but also in their houses, not so as to worship them but to call to mind whatever heavenly idea they stood for. Hence it was that in Egypt and elsewhere they used images of calves, oxen, and snakes, and even those of children, old men, and young women. For calves and oxen meant the affections and powers of the natural side of a person, snakes the prudence of people who rely on their senses; children meant innocence and charity, old men wisdom, young women affections for truth, and so on. Once the knowledge of correspondences had been wiped out their descendants started to

imagines et simulachra ab antiquis posita, quia in templis, et juxta illa, colere ut sancta, et tandem ut numina. Similiter apud alias gentes, sicut apud Philisthaeos in Aschdodo Dagon, de quo 1 Sam.5:1 ad fin., qui superius fuit sicut homo, inferius sicut piscis, quae imago inventa fuit, quia homo significat intelligentiam et piscis scientiam, quae unum faciunt.

Inde erat quoque antiquis cultus in hortis et in lucis secundum arborum species, tum etiam super montibus et collibus, horti enim et luci significabant sapientiam et intelligentiam, et unaquaevis arbor aliquid illarum, sicut olea bonum amoris, vitis verum ex illo bono, cedrus bonum et verum rationale, et mons significabat caelum supremum, et collis caelum sub illo.

Quod scientia correspondentiarum permanserit apud plures orientales usque ad adventum Domini, constare potest ex sapientibus ab oriente qui venerunt ad Dominum cum natus est, quare illis praeivit stella, et illi secum tulerunt dona, aurum, thus, et myrrham, Matt.2:1,2,9-11. Stella enim quae praeivit significabat cognitionem e caelo, aurum significabat bonum caeleste, thus bonum spirituale, et myrrha bonum naturale, ex quibus tribus est omnis cultus.

Sed usque scientia correspondentiarum prorsus nulla fuit apud gentem Israeliticam et Judaicam, tametsi omnia cultus illorum, et omnia judicia et statuta illis per Mosen data, et omnia Verbi, erant merae correspondentiae. Causa erat quia illi corde idololatrae erant, et tales ut ne quidem scire vellent quod aliquid cultus illorum significaret caeleste et spirituale. Volebant enim ut illa omnia sancta essent ex se et cum illis, quare si illis caelestia et spiritualia detecta fuissent, non modo rejecissent illa sed etiam prophanavissent; quapropter caelum illis ita clausum fuit ut vix scirent quod vita aeterna daretur. Quod ita sit, manifeste patet ex eo quod non agnoscerent Dominum, tametsi universa Scriptura Sacra de Ipso prophetavit, et adventum Ipsius praedixit. Rejecerunt Ipsum propter illam solam causam, quia illos de regno caelesti, et non de regno terrestri, docuit, voluerunt enim Messiam qui illos super omnes gentes in universo mundo exaltaret, et non aliquem Messiam qui saluti eorum aeternae

---

34 et Adventum Ipsius *VR*: et Ipsum *SS*

worship as holy, and finally as deities, the images and statues their ancestors had erected, because they were in or near temples. The like of this happened among other nations, such as the Philistines in Ashdod. In their temple – as described in 1 Sam.5:1-end – they worshipped the image Dagon, the upper part of which was a human being, the lower part a fish, so designed because human being stands for intelligence and fish for knowledge, which together make a single entity.

This too was the reason why the ancients worshipped in gardens and plantations, depending on the species of tree, as well as on mountains and hills. Gardens and plantations meant wisdom and intelligence, and each tree meant some particular detail of them. For instance, the olive meant the goodness of love, the vine truth coming from that goodness, the cedar rational goodness and truth, a mountain the highest heaven, and a hill the heaven below this.

The fact that the science of correspondences was preserved among a number of eastern peoples right down to the Lord's coming can be established by the wise men from the east who came to visit the Lord at the time of His birth; therefore the star went before them, and they brought gifts with them, gold, frankincense, and myrrh, Matt.2:1,2,9-11. The star which went before them meant knowledge learned from heaven, gold celestial goodness, frankincense spiritual goodness, and myrrh natural goodness; it is these three kinds of goodness which are the source of all worship.

Nonetheless correspondences were totally unknown to the Israelite and Jewish nation, even though all the details of their worship, and all the judgments and laws given them through Moses, and everything in the Word were nothing but correspondences. The reason was that they were at heart idolatrous, and of such a character that they did not even want to know that anything in their worship had a celestial or spiritual meaning. They wanted all of this to exist with them and be by itself holy. If therefore the celestial and spiritual meanings had been revealed to them, they would have not only rejected them, but also profaned them. On account of this heaven was so closed to them that they scarcely knew there was an eternal life. The truth of this is perfectly plain from the fact that they failed to acknowledge the Lord, even though the whole Sacred Scripture was a prophecy about Him and foretold His coming. The only reason why they rejected Him was that He taught them about a kingdom in heaven, not one on earth; for they wanted a Messiah who would make them superior to all nations throughout the world, not one who would provide for their eternal salvation. What is more, though

consuleret. Praeterea affirmant quod Verbum in se contineat multa arcana, quae mystica vocantur, sed non scire volunt quod illa sint de Domino; at scire volunt cum dicitur quod illa sint de auro.

24 Quod scientia correspondentiarum, per quam datur sensus spiritualis Verbi, post ea tempora non detecta fuerit, fuit causa quia Christiani in primitiva ecclesia perquam simplices fuerunt ut coram illis non detegi potuerit, nam si detecta, illis nullius usus fuisset, nec intelligeretur. Post illorum tempora obortae sunt tenebrae super universum Christianum orbem ex dominio papali; et qui ex illo sunt, et in falsis ejus se confirmaverunt, non possunt nec volunt capere aliquod spirituale, ita quid correspondentia naturalium cum spiritualibus in Verbo, sic enim convincerentur quod Petrus non intelligatur per Petrum sed Dominus ut Petra, et quoque convincerentur quod Verbum usque ad intima sua Divinum esset, et quod dictamen Papae sit nullius rei respective. Post Reformationem autem, quia distinguere caeperunt inter fidem et charitatem, ac colere Deum sub tribus Personis, ita tres Deos, quos cogitarent unum, tunc veritates caelestes illis abscondebantur, ac si detectae fuissent, illas falsificavissent, et illas deduxissent ad solam fidem, et nullam illarum ad charitatem et amorem; sic etiam occlusissent sibi caelum.

25 Quod sensus spiritualis Verbi hodie a Domino detectus sit, est quia doctrina genuini veri nunc revelata est; et haec doctrina cum sensu spirituali Verbi concordat, et non alia. Ille sensus etiam significatur per apparitionem Domini in nubibus caeli cum gloria et virtute, Matt.24:30,31, in quo capite agitur de consummatione saeculi, per quam intelligitur ultimum tempus ecclesiae. Aperitio Verbi quoad sensum ejus spiritualem etiam promissa est in Apocalypsi; ille ibi intelligitur per equum album, et per caenam magnam, ad quam omnes invitantur, 19:11-18. Quod sensus spiritualis diu non agnoscetur, quod solum fit ab illis qui in falsis doctrinae sunt, imprimis de Domino, et ideo non admittunt vera, intelligitur in Apocalypsi per bestiam et per reges terrae, qui facturi bellum cum Sedente super equo albo, 19:19; per bestiam intelliguntur Pontificii, ut 17:3 ibi, et per reges terrae intelliguntur Reformati, qui in falsis doctrinae sunt.

they agree there are many ideas hidden within the Word, which they term mystic, they do not want to know that these relate to the Lord; they want to know only when someone says that they relate to gold.

24 The reason why the science of correspondences, which allows people to grasp the spiritual sense of the Word, was not made known after this period was that the Christians of the primitive church were very simple, so that it could not be made known to them, since, had it been, it would not have been understood and would have been no use to them. After their times darkness has arisen over the whole Christian world as a result of the Papal supremacy; and those subject to it who have firmly accepted its false notions have no ability nor any desire to learn about anything spiritual, consequently what the correspondence in the Word of natural things with spiritual realities is. If they did they would become convinced that not Peter but the Lord as Petra or the Rock is meant there by Peter, and they would also become convinced that the Word right to its inmost parts was Divine and that in comparison a decree of the Pope has no validity. Furthermore, because people, after the Reformation, began to separate faith and charity, as well as to worship God in three Persons, and so three Gods, whom they imagined to be one, heavenly truths were hidden from their eyes. If these had been disclosed to them they would have falsified them, subordinated them all to faith alone, and none to charity and love, and in so doing would also have closed heaven to themselves.

25 Why it is that the spiritual sense of the Word has been made known by the Lord at the present time is that teaching presenting genuine truth has been revealed, and this teaching alone, no other, accords with the spiritual sense of the Word. This sense is also meant by the Lord's appearing in the clouds of heaven in glory and power, Matt.24:30,31, in a chapter dealing with the close of the age, by which the final period of the church is meant. The promise of the opening of the Word as to its spiritual sense has been foretold also in the Book of Revelation, where it is meant by the white horse, and the great feast to which everyone is invited, 19:11-18. The fact that for a long time the spiritual sense will not be recognized – which is entirely due to those who, being steeped in the false ideas of their teachings, especially ideas about the Lord, do not therefore entertain true ideas – is what is meant by the beast and the kings of the earth who are going to make war with Him seated on the white horse, 19:19. The beast means the Papists, as at 17:3 of that book, and the kings of the earth the Reformed, who are steeped in the false ideas of their teachings.

26 v **Quod sensus spiritualis Verbi non alicui posthac detur, nisi qui in genuinis veris a Domino est.** Causa haec est quia nemo potest sensum spiritualem videre nisi a solo Domino et nisi in genuinis veris ab Ipso sit. Sensus enim spiritualis Verbi agit de solo Domino et de Ipsius regno, et ille sensus est in quo sunt angeli Ipsius in caelo, est enim Divinum Ipsius Verum ibi. Hoc homo violare potest si in scientia correspondentiarum est et per illam vult sensum spiritualem Verbi ex propria intelligentia explorare, nam ex aliquibus correspondentiis sibi notis potest sensum ejus pervertere, et illum ad confirmandum etiam falsum trahere, et hoc foret violare Divinum Verum, et quoque caelum. Quare si quis a se et non a Domino sensum illum aperire vult, clauditur caelum; quo clauso, homo aut nihil veri videt aut spiritualiter insanit.

Causa etiam est quia Dominus per Verbum unumquemque docet, et docet ex illis veris quae apud hominem sunt, et non immediate nova infundit, quare nisi homo in Divinis veris sit, aut si modo in paucis veris et simul in falsis, potest ex his falsificare vera, ut quoque fit a quovis haeretico quoad ipsum sensum literae Verbi, ut notum est. Ne itaque aliquis in sensum spiritualem Verbi intret, ac genuinum verum, quod illius sensus est, pervertat, custodiae a Domino positae sunt, quae in Verbo per cherubos intelliguntur. Quod custodiae sint positae, hoc mihi ita repraesentatum est –

Datum est videre magnas crumenas, apparentes sicut sacci, in quibus reconditum fuit argentum in multa copia; et quia apertae erant, perceptum est sicut unusquisque posset argentum ibi repositum depromere, imo diripere; sed juxta crumenas illas sedebant bini angeli, qui custodes. Locus ubi repositae erant apparebat instar praesepis in stabulo; in camera proxima visae sunt virgines modestae, cum uxore casta; et prope illam cameram stabant bini infantes, et dictum est quod cum illis non infantiliter sed sapienter ludendum sit. Postea apparebat scortum, tum equus jacens mortuus.

Quibus visis, instructus sum quod per illa repraesentatus sit sensus literae Verbi, in quo sensus spiritualis. Magnae illae crumenae argento plenae significabant cognitiones veri in multa copia. Quod apertae essent, et tamen ab angelis custoditae, significabat

14 veri *VR*: *om SS*
21 ac *VR*: aut *SS*
26 *om* in *SS*[1]

26   v **The spiritual sense of the Word will in future be granted only to those who are in possession of genuine truths from the Lord.** The reason why is this. No one can see the spiritual sense, unless the Lord alone enables them and they are in possession of genuine truths received from Him. For the spiritual sense of the Word has to do with the Lord alone and His kingdom. That is the sense known to His angels in heaven, since it contains His Divine Truth. People who know the science of correspondences and want to use their own intelligence to explore the spiritual sense of the Word can do violence to this Divine Truth. For a knowledge of a few correspondences will enable them to corrupt that sense and even misapply it to proving false propositions. This would be to do violence to Divine Truth, and also to heaven. Therefore if any people wish to lay bare that sense, relying on themselves instead of on the Lord, heaven is closed to them, and this results in their being unable to see any truth at all, or in their becoming spiritually deranged.

Another reason is that the Lord teaches every person by means of the Word, and uses the truths they already have rather than directly implanting new ones. Therefore, if people are not in possession of Divine truths, or only a few truths accompanied by false notions, they can use these to falsify the truths. This too, as it is well known, is what any heretic does with the literal sense of the Word. So to prevent anyone coming into possession of the spiritual sense and perverting the genuine truth that sense contains, the Lord has established guards, who are meant by the cherubim in the Word. The establishment of the guards has been represented to me in the following way – 2

I was given to see great money bags, they looked like sacks, in which a large sum of money was stored. Since they were open it looked as though anyone could help themselves to the money stored there, or even steal it. But a pair of angels sat next to the money bags, to guard them. The place where they were put looked like a manger in a stable. In the next room some modest young women were to be seen accompanied by a respectable wife. Near the room stood two young children, and I was told they were to be played with not as children but those who were wise. Afterwards a whore appeared, and a horse lying dead. 3

Having seen all this I was informed that it represented the literal sense of the Word, which contains the spiritual sense. The large bags full of money meant an abundant supply of knowledge of truth. Their being open but guarded by angels meant anyone can 4

quod quisque posset inde cognitiones veri desumere, sed quod caveatur ne aliquis sensum spiritualem, in quo merae veritates sunt, falsificet. Praesepe in stabulo, in quo jacebant crumenae, significabat instructionem spiritualem pro intellectu; hoc significat praesepe, quia equus, qui inde edit, significat intellectum. Virgines modestae quae in camera proxima visae sunt significabant affectiones veri, et uxor casta conjunctionem boni et veri. Infantes significabant innocentiam sapientiae inibi; erant angeli e tertio caelo, qui omnes apparent sicut infantes. Scortum cum equo mortuo significabat falsificationem Verbi a multis hodie, per quam omnis intellectus veri perit; scortum significat falsificationem ac equus mortuus intellectum veri nullum.

---

5   significat intellectum SS^3: intellectum SS^1, SS^2, VR; significat intellectum Verbi AR
10 Verbi AR, SS: veri VR
11 significat AR, SS^1, VR: significabat SS^2, SS^3

help themselves to the knowledge of truth from this source, but precautions are taken to prevent anyone falsifying the spiritual sense, which contains bare truths. The manger in a stable, in which the large bags were lying, meant spiritual instruction for the understanding; this is the meaning of a manger because a horse, which eats from it, means the understanding. The modest young women seen in the next room meant the affections for truth, and the respectable wife the joining of goodness and truth. The young children meant the innocence of wisdom within this; they were angels from the third heaven, who all look like young children. The whore with the dead horse meant the falsification of the Word practised by many at the present time, which destroys all understanding of truth; whore means falsification, and dead horse an understanding of truth reduced to none at all.

Quod sensus literae Verbi sit basis, continens, et firmamentum sensus spiritualis et caelestis ejus

27. In omni Divino opere est primum, medium, et ultimum, ac primum vadit per medium ad ultimum, et sic existit et subsistit; inde ultimum est *basis*. Tum, primum est in medio et per medium in ultimo; ita ultimum est *continens*. Et quia ultimum est continens et basis, est etiam *firmamentum*.

28. Ab erudito comprehenditur quod illa tria nominari possint Finis, Causa, et Effectus, tum Esse, Fieri, et Existere, et quod finis sit esse, causa sit fieri, et effectus sit existere, consequenter quod in omni re completa sit trinum, quod vocatur Primum, Medium, et Ultimum, tum Finis, Causa, et Effectus, et quoque Esse, Fieri, et Existere. Cum haec comprehenduntur, etiam comprehenditur quod omne Divinum opus in ultimo sit completum et perfectum, et quoque quod in ultimo, quod trinum est, sit omne, quia in illo priora simul.

29. Ex eo est quod per tria in Verbo in sensu spirituali intelligatur completum et perfectum, tum omne simul; et quia haec per illum numerum significantur, ideo toties in Verbo adhibetur, quoties tale designatur. Ut in his, quod Esaias iret nudus et discalceatus **tres annos**, Esai.20:3. Quod Jehovah **ter** vocaverit Samuelem, et quod Samuel **ter** cucurrerit ad Eli, et quod Eli **tertia vice** intellexerit, 1 Sam.3:1-8. Quod Jonathan diceret ad Davidem quod occultaret se in agro **tribus diebus**; quod Jonathan postea ad latus lapidis jacularetur **tres sagittas**; et quod post illud David se incurvaret **tribus vicibus** coram Jonathane, 1 Sam.20:5,12-42. Quod Elias se mensus sit super filium viduae **tribus vicibus**, 1 Reg.17:21. Quod Elias jusserit ut funderent aquam super holocaustum **tribus vicibus**, 1 Reg.18:34. Quod Jesus dixerit quod regnum caelorum sit simile fermento, quod accipiens mulier abscondidit in **tribus satis**, donec fermentaretur totum, Matt.13:33. Quod Jesus dixerit

22 quod VR: om SS

The literal sense of the Word is the basis, container, and support of its spiritual and celestial senses

27   Every Divine work contains a first, middle, and last. The first passes through the middle to the last, and so it comes into and remains in existence; and the last is consequently its *basis*. The first is also present in the middle, and through this in the last; so the last is a *container*. And because the last is a container and basis it is also a *support*.

28   An educated reader will grasp that those three may be termed End, Cause, and Effect, and also Being, Becoming, and Coming-into-being; the end is being, the cause is becoming, and the effect is coming-into-being. Consequently, everything contains a triad called First, Middle, and Last, or End, Cause, and Effect, or else Being, Becoming, and Coming-into-being. When this is grasped it will also be grasped that every Divine work is complete and perfect in its last, and also that the last, which is a triad, contains everything, because the prior two are simultaneously present in it.

29   This is why three in the Word means in the spiritual sense complete and perfect, as well as the whole taken together. The meaning of the number three explains why it is used so many times in the Word, whenever anything of this sort is mentioned. For instance, Isaiah was told to go naked and barefoot for **three years**, Isa.20:3. Jehovah called Samuel **three times**, and Samuel **three times** ran to Eli, and **the third time** Eli understood, 1 Sam.3:1-8. Jonathan told David to hide in the country for **three days**; Jonathan later shot **three arrows** beside the stone, and after that David bowed down **three times** before Jonathan, 1 Sam.20:5,12-42. Elijah stretched himself **three times** over the widow's son, 1 Kings 17:21. Elijah ordered them to pour water on the burnt offering **three times**, 1 Kings 18:34. Jesus said that the kingdom of the heavens is like yeast, which a woman took and hid in **three measures** of meal, until the whole should be leavened, Matt.13:33. Jesus said to Peter that he would deny Him

ad Petrum quod **ter** abnegaturus sit Ipsum, Matt.26:34. Quod Dominus **ter** dixerit Petro, Amasne Me? Joh.21:15-17. Quod Jonas fuerit in ventre ceti **tribus diebus et tribus noctibus**, Jon.2:1. Quod Jesus dixerit quod Templum dissolverent, et Ipse illud per **tres dies** aedificaret, Matt.26:61. Quod Jesus in Gethsemane **tribus vicibus** oraverit, Matt.26:39-44. Quod Jesus **tertio die** resurrexerit, Matt.28:1. Praeter multis aliis in locis, ubi tria nominantur; et nominantur ubi agitur de opere finito et perfecto, quia hoc per illum numerum significatur.

30   Haec praemissa sunt propter sequentia, ut ea intellectualiter comprehendantur, hic nunc ut comprehendatur quod sensus naturalis Verbi, qui est sensus literae ejus, sit basis, continens, et firmamentum sensus spiritualis et sensus caelestis ejus.

31   Quod in Verbo tres sensus sint, supra n.6 et 19, dictum est, tum quod sensus caelestis sit primus ejus, sensus spiritualis medius ejus, et sensus naturalis ultimus ejus. Inde homo rationalis concludere potest quod primum Verbi, quod est caeleste, vadat per medium ejus, quod est spirituale, ad ultimum ejus, quod est naturale; et quod sic ultimum ejus sit *basis*; tum quod primum ejus, quod est caeleste, sit in medio ejus, quod est spirituale, et per hoc in ultimo ejus, quod est naturale; et quod inde ultimum ejus, quod est naturale, et est sensus literae Verbi, sit *continens*, et quia est continens, et basis, quod etiam sit *firmamentum*.

32   Sed quomodo haec fiunt, non paucis dici potest. Sunt etiam arcana, in quibus sunt angeli caeli, quae in transactionibus in praefatione ad **Doctrinam de Domino** memoratis, quae erunt ex Sapientia Angelica, de **Divina Providentia**, **Omnipotentia, Omnipraesentia, Omniscientia**, de **Divino Amore et de Divina Sapientia**, tum de **Vita**, quantum fieri potest, evolventur. Satis nunc est quod ex supradictis possit concludi quod Verbum, quod est ipsum Divinum opus pro salvatione humani generis, quoad sensum ejus ultimum, qui est naturalis et vocatur sensus literae, sit binorum sensuum interiorum basis, continens, et firmamentum.

33   Ex his sequitur quod Verbum absque sensu literae ejus foret sicut palatium absque fundamento, ita sicut palatium in aere et non super terra, quod modo foret umbra

---

5   Matt.26:61 *SS*[3], *VR*[2]: Matt.26:31 *SS*[1], *SS*[2], *VR*[1]; Joh.2:19, vide etiam Matt.26:61 *VR*[3]

three times, Matt.26:34. The Lord said **three times** to Peter, Do you love Me? John 21:15-17. Jonah was in the belly of the whale **three days and three nights**, Jon.1:17. Jesus said that they would destroy the temple and He would rebuild it in **three days**, Matt.26:61. In Gethsemane Jesus prayed **three times**, Matt.26:39-44. Jesus rose again on **the third day**, Matt.28:1. There are many other places where the number three is mentioned, in each case where a finished and perfect work is described, because this is the meaning of that number.

30 These considerations have been presented first for the sake of things to follow, so that people may grasp them with their understanding, and now, at this point, so that they may grasp that the natural sense of the Word, that is, its literal sense, is the basis, container, and support of its spiritual sense and celestial sense.

31 It has been stated above, in §6 and §19, that in the Word there are three senses, and that the celestial sense is its first sense, spiritual sense its middle one, and natural sense its last. From this anyone using their reason may see that the first of the Word, which is celestial, passes through its middle, which is spiritual, to its last, which is natural, and that its last is therefore a **basis**. They may also see that its first, which is celestial, is within its middle, which is spiritual, and through this within its last, which is natural; consequently that its last, which is natural and is the literal sense of the Word, is a **container**, and being a container and basis is also a **support**.

32 But how these things come about cannot be explained briefly. They are, in truth, arcana which angels in heaven know about, and they will be explained, as far as possible, in the subjects mentioned in the preface to **Teaching concerning the Lord**. These will draw on Angelic Wisdom concerning **Divine Providence**, **Omnipotence, Omnipresence, Omniscience**, concerning **Divine Love and Wisdom**, and also concerning **Life**. It is enough for now if people are enabled to see from what has been stated above that the Word, which is fundamentally a Divine work for the salvation of the human race, is in respect of its last sense – which is natural and is called the literal sense – the basis, container, and support of the two inner senses.

33 It follows from this that the Word without its literal sense would be like a palace without any foundations, a palace built not on land but in the air, which would be a mere evanescent shadow of

ejus, quae evanesceret. Tum quod Verbum absque sensu literae ejus foret sicut templum in quo plura sancta sunt, et in medio ejus adytum, absque tecto et pariete, quae sunt continentia ejus; quae si abessent vel si auferrentur, sancta ejus a furibus diriperentur, aut a bestiis terrae et a volucribus caeli violarentur, et sic dissiparentur. Similiter foret sicut tabernaculum – in cujus intimo fuit Arca Faederis, ac in medio ejus candelabrum aureum, altare aureum super quo suffimenta, tum mensa super qua panes facierum, quae erant sancta ejus – absque ultimis suis, quae erant aulaea et vela. Imo foret Verbum, absque sensu literae ejus, sicut corpus humanum absque integumentis, quae vocantur cutes, et absque sustentaculis, quae vocantur ossa. Absque his et illis diffluerent omnia interiora ejus. Ac foret sicut cor et pulmo in thorace absque integumento suo, quod vocatur pleura, et sustentaculis suis, quae vocantur costae. Aut sicut cerebrum absque integumento suo, quod vocatur dura mater, et absque communi tegumento, continente, et firmamento suo, quod vocatur cranium. Simile foret cum Verbo absque sensu literae ejus; quare dicitur apud Esaiam, quod Jehovah creet super omni gloria obtegumentum, 4:5.

34   Simile foret cum caelis, ubi sunt angeli, absque mundo ubi sunt homines. Humanum genus est basis, continens, et firmamentum illorum, et apud homines et in illis est Verbum. Omnes enim caeli distincti sunt in duo regna, quae vocantur regnum caeleste et regnum spirituale; haec duo regna fundantur super regno naturali, in quo sunt homines. Similiter itaque Verbum, quod apud homines et in hominibus est. Quod caeli angelici distincti sint in duo regna, caeleste et spirituale, videatur in opere **De Caelo et Inferno**, n.20-28.

35   Quod prophetae Veteris Testamenti repraesentaverint Dominum quoad Verbum, et per id significaverint doctrinam ecclesiae ex Verbo, et quod inde vocati sint Filii hominis, in **Doctrina de Domino**, n.28, ostensum est, ex quo sequitur quod illi, per varia quae passi sunt et sustinuerunt, repraesentaverint violentiam sensui literae Verbi a Judaeis illatam, ut quod Esaias Propheta exueret saccum desuper lumbis suis, et exueret calceum desuper pede suo, ac iret nudus et discalceatus tres annos, Esai.20:2,3. Similiter, quod Ezechiel Propheta novaculam tonsorum traduceret super caput et super barbam, et tertiam partem combureret in medio urbis, tertiam percuteret gladio, et tertiam dispergeret in ventum, et

a palace. The Word without its literal sense would be like a church containing a number of sacred objects and in its centre a sanctuary, but devoid of the roof and walls which hold it together. If these were missing or removed the sacred objects would be stolen by thieves or ruined by land animals and birds of the air, and thus scattered. It would be like the tabernacle – in the inmost part of which was the Ark of the Covenant, and in its midst a golden lampstand, a golden altar bearing incense, and a table with the loaves of the presence on it, which were its sacred objects – if this were stripped of its outer covering, that is, its curtains and its veils. Rather, the Word without its literal sense would resemble the human body without an outer covering called the skin or a framework called the bones. If deprived of these two all the contents of the body would fall apart. Again it would be like heart and lungs in the chest devoid of their covering called the pleura, and their supports called the ribs. Or like the brain without its covering called the dura mater and without its general covering, container, and support called the skull. That is what the Word would be like without its literal sense, and this is why it says in Isaiah that Jehovah creates a covering over all glory, 4:5.

34   It is also what the heavens, where angels are, would be like without the world, where people are. The human race is their basis, container, and support; and the Word exists with and within people. For all the heavens are divided into two kingdoms, called the celestial kingdom and the spiritual kingdom, and these two kingdoms are based on the natural kingdom in which people are. It is therefore similarly so with the Word existing with and within people. Regarding the division of the angelic heavens into two kingdoms, celestial and spiritual, see the work **Heaven and Hell**, §§20-28.

35   It was shown in §28 of **Teaching concerning the Lord** that the Old Testament prophets represented the Lord in respect of the Word and as a consequence served to mean the teachings of the church derived from the Word, and for this reason they were called Sons of man. It follows from this that the various experiences they underwent and endured represented the violence done by the Jews to the literal sense of the Word. Isaiah the prophet, for instance, had to remove the sackcloth from over his loins and to remove the shoes from over his feet, and to go naked and barefoot for three years, Isa.20:2,3. In a similar way Ezekiel the prophet had to pass a barber's razor over his head and beard, burn a third in the middle of the city, strike a third with a sword, scatter a third to the wind, bind a small

parum ex illis alligaret in alis, et tandem projiceret in medium ignis et combureret, Ezech.5:1-4.

Quia prophetae repraesentaverunt Verbum, et inde significaverunt doctrinam ecclesiae ex Verbo, ut supra dictum est, et quia per caput significatur sapientia ex Verbo, inde per capillitium et per barbam significabatur ultimum veri. Quia hoc per illa significabatur, ideo signum grandis luctus, et quoque grande dedecus erat, *calvitium* sibi inducere, et quoque *calvus* apparere. Propter illam et non aliam causam erat quod Propheta abraderet capillos capitis sui et barbam, ut per id repraesentaret statum Ecclesiae Judaicae quoad Verbum. Propter illam et non aliam causam discerpti sunt quadraginta duo pueri a duabus ursis, *qui Elisaeum vocaverunt calvum*, 2 Reg.2:23,24; nam propheta repraesentabat Verbum, ut prius dictum est, et calvum significabat illud absque suo sensu ultimo.

Quod Naziraei repraesentaverint Dominum quoad Verbum in suis ultimis, in sequente articulo, n.49, videbitur, ideo statutum fuit pro illis ut crescere facerent comam et nihil ejus abraderent. Naziraeus etiam in lingua Hebraea significat comam. Statutum etiam fuit pro sacerdote magno, quod non raderet caput, Lev.21:10; similiter pro patrefamilias, Lev.21:5.

Inde erat quod calvitium illis grande dedecus esset, ut constare potest ex his –

In omnibus capitibus calvities, et omnis barba rasa. Esai.15:2; Jer.48:37.
Super omnibus faciebus pudor, et in omnibus capitibus calvities. Ezech.7:18.
Omne caput decalvatum, et omnis humerus depilatus. Ezech.29:18.
Ascendere faciam super omnes lumbos saccum, et super omne caput calvitiem. Amos 8:10.
Calvitiem induc, et tonde te propter filios delitiarum tuarum; et dilata calvitiem, quia migrarunt a te. Mic.1:16.

Hic per calvitiem inducere et dilatare significatur vera Verbi in ultimis ejus falsificare; quibus falsificatis, ut factum est a Judaeis, totum Verbum destructum est. Nam ultima Verbi sunt fulcra et sustentacula ejus, imo unaquaevis vox est fulcrum et sustentaculum veritatum caelestium et spiritualium ejus. Quia capillitium significat verum in ultimis,

---

30 induc SS^3: indue SS^1, SS^2
32 inducere SS^3: induere SS^1, SS^2

part of them in the skirts of his robe, and finally cast some in the middle of the fire and burn them, Ezek.5:1-4.

Because the prophets represented the Word and as a consequence served to mean the teaching of the church derived from the Word, as shown above, and because wisdom derived from the Word is meant by the head, the hair on it and the beard served to mean truth in the outermost form it takes. Such being the meaning of hair and beard, to make oneself **bald**, and to be seen **bald**, was an indication of deep mourning, or else of great shame. It was for the following and no other reason that prophets shaved off their hairs on the head and their beard, to represent the state of the Jewish church in respect of the Word. For this and no other reason were the forty-two boys **who called Elisha baldhead** torn apart by the two bears, 2 Kings 2:23,24; for a prophet represented the Word, as stated before, and baldhead meant it devoid of its outermost sense.

In the next section, at §49, it will be seen that Nazirites represented the Lord in regard of the outermost aspects of the Word, and therefore they were required to let the hair grow on their head and not shave any of it off; furthermore, Nazirite in Hebrew means the hair of the head. The high priest too was forbidden to shave his head, Lev.21:10; and so was the chief of a household, Lev.21:5.

So it was that for them baldness was a mark of great shame, as the following places make clear –

On all heads there is baldness, and every beard is shaved off. Isa.15:2; Jer.48:37.
On all faces there will be shame, and on all heads baldness. Ezek.7:18.
Every head bald, and every shoulder rubbed bare[1]. Ezek.29:18.
I will cause sackcloth to come up over all loins, and baldness over every head. Amos 8:10.
Make yourself bald, and shave yourself because of the children of your delight; and extend the baldness, for they have departed from you. Mic.1:16.

The self-made baldness and extending of it in this verse means the falsifying of the truths of the Word in its last and outermost parts. Once they had been falsified, as was done by the Jews, the Word had been destroyed. For the outermost parts of the Word are its underpinnings and supports, or rather each expression is an underpinning and support of its celestial and spiritual truths. Because

---

1   lit. *de-haired*

ideo in mundo spirituali omnes qui contemnunt Verbum, et sensum literae ejus falsificant, apparent calvi, at qui honorant et amant illum apparent in decentibus comis. De hac re videatur etiam infra, n.49.

36 Verbum in sensu ultimo seu naturali, qui est sensus literae ejus, significatur etiam per murum sanctae Hierosolymae, cujus structura erat jaspis, perque fundamenta muri, quae erant lapides pretiosi, tum etiam per portas, quae erant margaritae, Apoc.19:18-21; nam per Hierosolymam significatur ecclesia quoad doctrinam. Sed de his plura in sequente articulo.

Ex allatis nunc constare potest quod sensus literae Verbi, qui est naturalis, sit basis, continens, et firmamentum sensuum interiorum ejus, qui sunt sensus spiritualis et caelestis.

the hair of the head means truth in outermost parts all in the spiritual world who treat the Word with contempt and falsify its literal sense are seen bald, whereas those who show respect for it and love it are seen having lovely hair. See also below, at §49, on this matter.

36   The Word in its outermost or natural sense, that is, its literal sense, is also meant by the wall of the holy Jerusalem, which was built of jasper, and by the foundations of the wall, which were precious stones, as well as by the gates, which were pearls, Rev.19:18-21. For Jerusalem means the church in respect of its teaching. But more about these meanings will appear in the next section.

What has now been mentioned shows that the literal sense of the Word, which is natural, is the basis, container, and support of its inner senses, that is, the spiritual sense and the celestial.

Quod Divinum Verum in sensu literae Verbi sit in suo pleno, in suo sancto, et in sua potentia

37 Quod Verbum in suo sensu literae sit in suo pleno, in suo sancto, et in sua potentia, est quia bini sensus priores seu interiores, qui vocantur spiritualis et caelestis, in sensu naturali, qui est sensus literae, sunt simul, ut supra, n.31, dictum est. Sed quomodo sunt simul, paucis nunc dicetur.

38 Datur in caelo et in mundo ordo successivus et ordo simultaneus. In ordine successivo succedit et sequitur unum post alterum, a supremis usque ad infima; in ordine autem simultaneo est unum juxta alterum, ab intimis usque ad extima. Ordo successivus est sicut columna cum gradibus a summo ad imum, at ordo simultaneus est sicut opus cohaerens cum peripheriis a centro ad superficiem.

Nunc dicetur quomodo ordo successivus fit in ultimo ordo simultaneus. Fit hoc modo: suprema ordinis successivi fiunt intima ordinis simultanei, ac infima ordinis successivi fiunt extima ordinis simultanei; est comparative sicut columna graduum subsidens fit corpus cohaerens in plano. Ita formatur simultaneum a successivo, et hoc in omnibus et singulis mundi naturalis, et in omnibus et singulis mundi spiritualis, nam ubivis est primum, medium, et ultimum, ac primum per medium tendit et vadit ad suum ultimum.

Nunc ad Verbum: caeleste, spirituale, et naturale procedunt a Domino in ordine successivo, et in ultimo sunt in ordine simultaneo; ita nunc sensus caelestis et spiritualis Verbi sunt in sensu ejus naturali simul. Dum hoc comprehenditur, videri potest quomodo sensus naturalis Verbi, qui est sensus literae ejus, est basis, continens, et firmamentum sensus spiritualis et caelestis ejus, tum quomodo Divinum Bonum et Divinum Verum in sensu literae Verbi est in suo pleno, in suo sancto, et in sua potentia.

The Divine Truth in the literal sense of the Word is in its fullness, holiness, and power

37   The Word in its literal sense is in its fullness, holiness, and power because the two prior or inward senses, called the spiritual and celestial senses, are simultaneously present in the natural or literal sense, as stated above, §31. But at this point a brief explanation showing how they are simultaneously present is necessary.

38   There are in heaven and in the world two kinds of order, successive and simultaneous. In the case of successive order one thing succeeds or follows after another, from those which are highest to those that are lowest; but in the case of simultaneous order, one stands alongside another, from those which are inmost to those which are outermost. Successive order is like a column with steps from top to bottom; but simultaneous order is like an object made up of cohering rings, from the centre out to the circumference.

Now it must be explained how at the lowest level successive order becomes simultaneous. It is like this. The highest levels of a successive order become the inmost parts of a simultaneous order, and the lowest levels of a successive order become the outermost parts of a simultaneous order. This can be illustrated by a stepped column subsiding to become a coherent object in a single plane. So the simultaneous is formed from the successive, and this operates in every single thing in the natural world, and in every single one in the spiritual world; for everywhere there is a first, middle, and last, and the first reaches out through the middle and advances towards its last.

2

Now let this be applied to the Word. The celestial, spiritual, and natural proceed from the Lord in successive order, and are in simultaneous order at the lowest level. So that is how the celestial and spiritual senses of the Word are simultaneously present in its natural sense. Once this has been grasped it can be seen how the natural sense of the Word, which is its literal sense, is the basis, container, and support of its spiritual and celestial senses, as well as how Divine Goodness and Divine Truth are present in the literal sense of the Word in their fullness, holiness, and power.

39 Ex his constare potest quod Verbum sit ipsum Verbum in suo sensu literae, in hoc enim intus est spiritus et vita; sensus spiritualis est ejus spiritus, et sensus caelestis est ejus vita. Hoc est quod Dominus dicit,

Verba quae Ego loquor vobis, spiritus et vita sunt. Joh.6:63.

Dominus verba Sua coram mundo, et in sensu naturali loquutus est. Sensus spiritualis et sensus caelestis non sunt Verbum absque sensu naturali, qui est sensus literae, sunt enim sicut spiritus et vita absque corpore, et sunt. ut prius, n.33, dictum est, sicut palatium cui deest basis.

40 Vera sensus literae Verbi quoad partem non sunt nuda vera sed sunt apparentiae veri, ac sicut similitudines et comparationes, desumptae ex talibus quae in natura sunt, ita quae accommodata et adaequata sunt captui simplicium et quoque infantum. Sed quia sunt correspondentiae, sunt genuini veri receptacula et habitacula, et sunt sicut vasa quae includunt et continent, quemadmodum poculum chrystallinum includit nobile vinum, et quemadmodum patina argentea continet edules cibos. Et sunt quemadmodum vestes quae amiciunt, ut fasciae infantem, ac decori amictus virginem. Sunt etiam sicut scientifica naturalis hominis, quae in se comprehendunt perceptiones et affectiones veri spiritualis hominis. Ipsa nuda vera, quae includuntur, continentur, investiuntur, et comprehenduntur, sunt in Verbi sensu spirituali, et nuda bona sunt in ejus sensu caelesti. Sed hoc e Verbo illustretur.

Dixit Jesus,

Vae vobis, Scribae et Pharisaei, quia purgatis exterius poculi et patinae, interiora vero sunt plena rapina et intemperantia. Pharisaee caece, purga prius interius poculi et patinae, ut sit etiam exterius mundum. Matt.23:25,26.

Hic loquutus est Dominus per ultima quae sunt continentia; et dixit poculum et patinam. Et per poculum intelligitur vinum, ac per vinum verum Verbi; et per patinam intelligitur cibus, ac per cibum bonum Verbi. Per purgare internum poculi et patinae intelligitur purificare interiora, quae sunt voluntatis et cogitationis, ita amoris et fidei, per Verbum; per quod sic exterius mundum sit, intelligitur quod sic exteriora purificata

39   From all this it can be established that the Word in its literal sense is the real Word, for it contains in itself spirit and life, the spiritual sense being its spirit, and the celestial sense its life. This is what the Lord says,

The words which I speak to you are spirit and life. John 6:63.

For the Lord uttered His words in the world, and in their natural sense. The spiritual sense and celestial sense without the natural or literal sense are not the Word, for that would be like spirit and life without a body; and they are, as said before, at §33, like a palace with no foundations under it.

40   The truths in the literal sense of the Word are in part not bare truths but appearances of truth. They are like similes and comparative analogies taken from appearances in the natural world. Thus they are adapted and brought down to the level at which they may be understood by simple people and even young children. But because they are correspondences they serve to receive and make a home for genuine truth. They are, so to speak, vessels which hold and contain, like a crystal cup holding vintage wine, or a silver salver containing tempting foods. They are like the garments that clothe people, for instance swathing bands clothing an infant, and pretty dresses a girl. They are also like the facts stored in the memory on the natural level of the human mind, which include the person's perceptions of affections for spiritual truth. The bare truths themselves which are wrapped, contained, clothed, and grasped exist in the spiritual sense of the Word, and the bare forms of goodness exist in its celestial sense. But illustrations must be given from the Word. Jesus said,   2

Woe to you, Scribes and Pharisees, because you clean the outside of the cup and dish, but the insides are full of robbery and intemperance. You blind Pharisee, clean first the inside of the cup and dish, so that the outside too may be clean. Matt.23:25,26.

When the Lord said this He used images of outward things that are containers; and He spoke about the cup and dish. Wine is meant by cup, and the truth of the Word by wine, while food is meant by dish, and the goodness of the Word by food. Cleaning the inside of the cup and dish means purifying the interior parts, the seats of will and thought, and so of love and faith, by means of the Word. So that in this way the outside may be clean means so that in this way

sint, quae sunt opera et loquela, nam haec ab illis trahunt suam essentiam. Adhuc, Jesus dixit,

Homo quidam erat dives qui induebatur purpura et bysso, et oblectabat se quotidie splendide; et pauper quidam erat nomine
5 Lazarus, qui projectus ad vestibulum ejus ulcerosus. Luc.16:19,20.

Hic etiam Dominus loquutus est per naturalia, quae erant correspondentiae et continebant spiritualia. Per hominem divitem intelligitur gens Judaica, quae dives vocatur quia habebat Verbum, in quo sunt divitiae spirituales; per
10 purpuram et byssum quibus indutus erat significatur bonum et verum Verbi, per purpuram bonum ejus et per byssum verum ejus; per oblectare se quotidie splendide significatur oblectatio quod illud haberet et legeret; per Lazarum pauperem intelliguntur gentes, quae non habebant Verbum. Quod illae
15 contemtae et rejectae a Judaeis essent, intelligitur per quod Lazarus ad vestibulum divitis esset projectus ulcerosus. Quod gentes per Lazarum intelligantur, erat quia gentes amabantur a Domino, sicut Lazarus, qui a mortuis resuscitatus est, amabatur a Domino, Joh.11:3,5,36, et vocatur Ipsius amicus,
20 Joh.11:11, et accumbebat ad mensam cum Domino, Joh.12:2.

Ex his binis locis patet quod vera et bona sensus literae Verbi sint sicut vasa et sicut vestes nudi veri et boni, quae in sensu spirituali et caelesti Verbi latent.

41   Quoniam Verbum in sensu literae tale est, sequitur
25 quod illi qui in Divinis veris sunt et in fide quod Verbum intus in suo sinu sanctum Divinum sit, et magis illi qui in fide sunt quod Verbum tale sit ex sensu spirituali et caelesti ejus, dum in illustratione a Domino legunt Verbum, videant Divina vera in luce naturali. Nam lux caeli, in qua est sensus
30 spiritualis Verbi, influit in lucem naturalem, in qua est sensus literae Verbi, ac hominis intellectuale, quod vocatur rationale, illuminat et facit ut videat et agnoscat Divina vera, ubi exstant et ubi latent. Haec cum luce caeli influunt apud quosdam, quandoque etiam cum nesciunt.
35 42   Quoniam Verbum nostrum in intimo suo sinu, ex sensu caelesti ejus, est sicut flamma quae accendit, et in medio suo sinu, ex sensu spirituali, est sicut lux quae illustrat, inde Verbum in ultimo suo sinu, ex sensu ejus naturali, in quo

14   quae SS: quia VR

the exteriors, works and utterance, are purified, for their essence is drawn from those interiors. Again Jesus said,

3

There was a certain rich man who dressed in purple and fine linen, and feasted magnificently every day; and there was a poor man named Lazarus, who lay in his entrance porch full of sores. Luke 16:19,20.

Here too the Lord spoke using images of natural things, which were correspondences and had a spiritual content. The rich man means the Jewish nation, which is called rich because it possessed the Word containing spiritual riches. The purple and fine linen which he wore means the goodness and truth of the Word, purple its goodness and fine linen its truth. Feasting magnificently every day means taking pleasure in having it and reading it. The poor man Lazarus means the gentiles who did not possess the Word. The contempt and rejection they suffered at the hands of the Jews are meant by Lazarus lying in the rich man's entrance porch full of sores. The reason the gentiles were meant by Lazarus was that the gentiles were loved by the Lord, just as Lazarus, who was revived after being dead, was loved by the Lord, John 11:3,5,36. He is also called His friend, John 11:11, and he reclined at table with the Lord, John 12:2.

4

These two passages show plainly that the truths and kinds of goodness in the literal sense of the Word are like vessels and garments serving to clothe bare truth and goodness, which lie hidden in the spiritual and celestial senses of the Word.

41   The Word being like this in its literal sense, it follows that those who possess Divine truths and believe that the Word inwardly in its depths is something holy and Divine, and more so those who believe that the Word is like this because of its spiritual and celestial senses, these people, when they read the Word and receive enlightenment from the Lord, see Divine truths by natural light. For the light of heaven, which illuminates the spiritual sense of the Word, exerts an influence on the natural light, which illuminates the literal sense of the Word and enlightens a person's intellectual, also called rational, faculty, enabling it to see and recognize Divine truths, whether plain to view or hidden. The light of heaven has this effect on people, sometimes without their even knowing it.

42   The celestial sense at the very heart of our Word makes it like a flame setting on fire, and its spiritual sense at the intermediate level like a light giving illumination. Consequently at its outermost level

bini interiores sunt, est sicut rubinus et adamas – ex flamma caelesti sicut rubinus et ex luce spirituali sicut adamas. Quia tale est Verbum in suo sensu literae ex transparentia, ideo Verbum in hoc sensu intelligitur per **fundamenta muri novae Hierosolymae**; per **Urim et Thumim** in ephodo Aharonis; per **hortum Edenis** in quo Rex Tyri fuerat; tum etiam per **aulaea et vela tabernaculi**; et per **externa templi Hierosolymitani**; at in ipsa gloria, per **Dominum cum transformatus est**.

43   Quod vera sensus literae Verbi intelligantur per fundamenta muri novae Hierosolymae, in Apocalypsi 21, sequitur ex eo quod per novam Hierosolymam intelligatur nova ecclesia quoad doctrinam, ut in **Doctrina de Domino**, n.62,63, ostensum est, quare per murum ejus et per muri fundamenta non aliud potest intelligi quam Verbi externum, quod est sensus literae ejus, nam ille est ex quo doctrina est, et per doctrinam ecclesia, et illa est sicut murus cum fundamentis qui urbem includit et tutatur. De muro novae Hierosolymae et de ejus fundamentis leguntur haec in Apocalypsi,

Angelus mensus est murum urbis Hierosolymae 144 cubitorum, quae erat mensura hominis, hoc est, angeli. Et murus habebat fundamenta duodecim, omni lapide pretioso exornata. Fundamentum primum jaspis, secundum sapphirus, tertium chalcedonius, quartum smaragdus, quintum sardonyx, sextum sardius, septimum chrysolithus, octavum beryllus, nonum topazius, decimum chrysoprasus, undecimum hyacinthus, duodecimum amethystus. 21:17-20.

Per numerum 144 significantur omnia vera et bona ecclesiae ex doctrina e sensu literae Verbi, similiter per duodecim, per hominem significatur intelligentia, per angelum Divinum verum ex quo illa, per mensuram quale illorum, per murum et per fundamenta ejus sensus literae Verbi, et per lapides pretiosos vera et bona Verbi in suo ordine, ex quibus doctrina et per doctrinam ecclesia.

---

4   novae *VR*: *om SS*
16 illa *SS*: ille *VR*

the natural sense containing the two inner senses makes it like a ruby or a diamond, the celestial flame like a ruby and the spiritual light like a diamond. Since the Word is like this in its literal sense by virtue of what shines through, this sense in the Word is what is meant by the **foundations of the wall of the new Jerusalem**; by the **Urim and Thummim** on Aaron's ephod; by the **garden of Eden** in which the King of Tyre had been; as well as by the **curtains and veils of the tabernacle**, and the **external features of the temple in Jerusalem**. But the Word in its glory was represented in **the Lord at His transfiguration**.

43 *The truths of the literal sense of the Word are meant by the foundations of the wall of the new Jerusalem* in the Book of Revelation 21. This follows from what was shown in **Teaching concerning the Lord**, §§62-63 – that by the new Jerusalem is meant a new church in respect of its teaching. Its wall and the foundations of the wall therefore cannot mean anything other than the outward aspect of the Word, that is, its literal sense; for it is this sense that teaching springs from, and through teaching the church. This teaching[1] is like a wall with its foundations, encompassing a city and making it secure. The description in the Book of Revelation of the wall of the new Jerusalem and its foundations is this,

The angel measured the wall of the city Jerusalem as 144 cubits, which is the measure of a human being, that is, an angel. And the wall had twelve foundations, decorated with every kind of precious stone. The first foundation was jasper, the second sapphire, the third chalcedony, the fourth emerald, the fifth sardonyx, the sixth sardius, the seventh chrysolite, the eighth beryl, the ninth topaz, the tenth chrysoprase, the eleventh turquoise, the twelfth amethyst. 21:17-20.

The number 144 means all the church's truths and forms of goodness that belong to its teaching derived from the literal sense of the Word, and so does twelve. Human being means intelligence, and angel Divine truth, the source of that intelligence. Measurement means the nature of them. The wall and its foundations mean the literal sense of the Word, and the precious stones the truths and forms of goodness of the Word in their proper order which are the source of the teaching, and by means of that teaching the church.

---

1   The Latin pronoun *illa* used here relates to the words immediately preceding, rendered *teaching the church*; but in a parallel passage (*VR* §217) the pronoun is *ille*, which refers further back to the words translated *literal sense*

44 Quod vera et bona sensus literae Verbi intelligantur per Urim et Thumim. Urim et Thumim erant super ephodo Aharonis, per cujus sacerdotium repraesentabatur Dominus quoad Divinum Bonum et quoad opus salvationis. Per vestes sacerdotii seu sanctitatis repraesentabatur Divinum Verum ex Divino Bono, per ephodum repraesentabatur Divinum Verum in suo ultimo, ita Verbum in sensu literae, nam hoc est Divinum Verum in suo ultimo, ut supra dictum est. Inde per duodecim lapides pretiosos, cum nominibus duodecim tribuum Israelis, quae fuerunt Urim et Thumim, repraesentabantur Divina Vera ex Divino Bono in omni complexu.

De his ita legitur apud Mosen,

Facient ephodum ex auro, hyacinthino, et purpura, coccineo dibapho, et xylino intertexto. Postea facies pectorale judicii, secundum opus ephodi. Et opplebis id oppleturis lapidis, quatuor ordines lapidis: pyropus, topazius, et smaragdus, primus ordo; chrysoprasus, sapphirus, et adamas, secundus ordo; cyanus, achates, et amethystus, tertius ordo; thalassius, sardius, et jaspis, quartus ordo. Lapides hi erunt juxta nomina filiorum Israelis; sculpturae sigilli juxta nomen suum erunt pro 12 tribubus. Et portabit Aharon super pectorali judicii Urim et Thumim, sintque super corde Aharonis, cum ingredietur ante Jehovam. Exod.28:6,15-21,29,30.

Quid per vestes Aharonis, ejus ephodum, pallium, tunicam, cidarim, baltheum, repraesentatum est, in **Arcanis Caelestibus** super eo capite explicatum est, ubi ostensum quod per ephodum repraesentatum sit Divinum Verum in suo ultimo; quod per lapides pretiosos ibi repraesentata sint vera pellucentia ex bono; per duodecim lapides pretiosos omnia vera ultima pellucentia ex bono amoris in suo ordine; per duodecim tribus Israelis, omnia ecclesiae; per pectorale Divinum Verum ex Divino Bono; per Urim et Thumim exsplendescentia Divini Veri ex Divino Bono in ultimis, Urim enim est ignis lucens et Thumim exsplendescentia in lingua angelica, et integritas in lingua Hebraea; tum quod responsa data sint per lucis variegationes, et simul tunc per tacitam perceptionem vel per vivam vocem; praeter plura.

13 auro SS^3, VR^3: om SS^1, SS^2, VR^1, VR^2
14 facies SS^3, VR^3: facient SS^1, SS^2, VR^1, VR^2
16 lapidis: lapis SS, VR

44 *The forms of truth and goodness belonging to the literal sense of the Word are meant by Urim and Thummim.* The Urim and Thummim were mounted on Aaron's ephod, and his priesthood represented the Lord in respect of Divine Goodness and the effecting of salvation. The garments of priesthood or of holiness represented Divine Truth coming from Divine Goodness, the ephod represented Divine Truth in its outermost form, that is, the literal sense of the Word, for this is Divine Truth in its outermost form, as stated above. Thus the twelve precious stones called the Urim and Thummim, which bore the names of the twelve tribes of Israel, represented Divine Truths coming from Divine Goodness and all that goes with them.

These things can be read about in the books of Moses, 2

They shall make the ephod of gold, violet, and purple, with doubledyed scarlet and lawn interwoven. Later you shall make the breastplate of judgment of similar workmanship to the ephod. And you shall fill it with settings for stones. There shall be four rows of stones: ruby, topaz, and emerald in the first row; chrysoprase, sapphire, and diamond in the second row; lapis lazuli, agate, and amethyst in the third row; aquamarine, sardius, and jasper in the fourth row. These stones shall answer to the names of the sons of Israel; the inscriptions on a seal shall have each the name of one of the 12 tribes. And Aaron shall wear upon the breastplate of judgment the Urim and Thummim; and let them be upon Aaron's heart, when he comes into the presence of Jehovah. Exod.28:6,15-21,29,30.

The representations of Aaron's garments – his ephod, mantle, tunic, 3 turban, and sash – have been explained in **Arcana Caelestia**, in the commentary on that chapter. It was there shown that the ephod represented Divine Truth in its outermost form; the precious stones represented the truths made pellucid by goodness; the twelve precious stones represented all the outermost forms of truth made pellucid by the goodness of love, in proper order; the twelve tribes of Israel represented the whole of the church. The breastplate represented Divine Truth coming from Divine Goodness; the Urim and Thummim represented the splendour of Divine Truth coming from Divine Goodness in its outermost form, for Urim is shining fire and Thummim is splendour in the language of angels, or wholeness in Hebrew. Again, replies were given by changes in the quality of light, accompanied by unspoken perception, or by direct speech; and there is much besides.

Ex quibus constare potest quod per hos lapides pretiosos etiam significata sint vera ex bono in sensu ultimo Verbi; nec per alia dantur responsa e caelo, quia in illo sensu est Divinum procedens in suo pleno. Quod lapides pretiosi et diademata significent Divina Vera in suis ultimis, qualia sunt vera sensus literae Verbi, patuit mihi manifeste ex lapidibus pretiosis et diadematibus in mundo spirituali apud angelos et spiritus ibi quos vidi illis indutos, et quoque in thecis illorum, et datum est scire quod illa corresponderent veris in ultimis, imo etiam quod inde sint et appareant. Quia haec per diademata et lapides pretiosos significantur, ideo illa etiam visa sunt Johanni super capite draconis, Apoc.12:3; super cornibus bestiae, Apoc.13:1; et lapides pretiosi super meretrice sedente super bestia coccinea, Apoc.17:4. Super illis visa sunt, quia per illos significantur ii in Christiano orbe apud quos est Verbum.

45   *Quod vera sensus literae Verbi intelligantur per lapides pretiosos in horto Edenis in quo, apud Ezechielem, Rex Tyri dicitur fuisse.* Legitur apud Ezechielem,

Rex Tyri, tu obsignans demensum tuum, plenus sapientia, et perfectus pulchritudine. In Eden horto Dei fuisti; omnis lapis pretiosus tegumentum tuum – rubinus, topazius, et adamas, tharscish, sardonyx, et jaspis, sapphirus, chrysoprasus, et smaragdus, et aurum. 28:12,13.

Per Tyrum in Verbo significantur cognitiones veri et boni; per regem significatur verum ecclesiae, per hortum Edenis significatur sapientia et intelligentia ex Verbo. Per lapides pretiosos significantur vera pellucentia ex bono, qualia sunt in sensu literae Verbi; et quia haec per illos lapides significantur, ideo vocantur tegumentum ejus. Quod sensus literae tegat interiora Verbi, videatur articulus praecedens.

46   *Quod sensus literae Verbi significetur per aulaea et vela tabernaculi.* Per tabernaculum repraesentatum est caelum et ecclesia, quare forma ejus a Jehovah super monte Sinai ostensa est. Inde per omnia quae in tabernaculo erant – quae erant candelabrum, altare aureum pro suffitu, et mensa super qua

These explanations establish that those precious stones also 4 stood for truths coming from goodness in the outermost sense of the Word. For this is the only source by which replies are given from heaven, because that sense contains the Divine which proceeds in all its fullness. That precious stones and jewels stand for Divine Truths in their outermost form, which is what truths belonging to the literal sense of the Word are, has become perfectly plain to me from the precious stones and the jewels in the spiritual world which I have seen angels and spirits wearing there, as well as seeing them resting in their caskets. I was led to realize that they corresponded to truths in their outermost form, or rather that they had their origin in and were manifestations of those truths. These being what jewels and precious stones stand for, the latter were therefore seen by John to be on the head of the dragon, Rev.12:3, and on the horns of the beast, Rev.13:1; and he saw precious stones on the prostitute sitting on the scarlet beast, Rev.17:4. They were seen to be on them because those three mean people in the Christian world with whom the Word exists.

45 *The truths belonging to the literal sense of the Word are meant by the precious stones in the Garden of Eden, in which, in Ezekiel, the King of Tyre is said to have been.* We read in Ezekiel,

King of Tyre, you who set your seal upon your measured space, full of wisdom and perfect in beauty. You were in Eden, God's garden; every kind of precious stone was your covering – ruby, topaz, and diamond, beryl, sardonyx, and jasper, sapphire, chrysoprase, and emerald, and gold. 28:12,13.

Tyre in the Word means recognitions of truth and goodness; king means the church's truth, garden of Eden wisdom and intelligence derived from the Word. Precious stones mean truths made pellucid by goodness, of the sort found in the literal sense of the Word. It is because these are meant by those stones that they are called its covering. The literal sense is a covering for the inward contents of the Word; see the previous section.[1]

46 *The literal sense of the Word is meant by the curtains and veils of the tabernacle.* The tabernacle was a representation of heaven and the church. That is why the design of it was made known by Jehovah on Mount Sinai. Thus all the contents of the tabernacle – the lampstand, the golden altar for incense, and the table with the loaves

1   ie §33

panes facierum – repraesentata et inde significata sunt sancta caeli et ecclesiae; ac per sanctum sanctorum, ubi erat Arca Faederis, repraesentatum et inde significatum est intimum caeli et ecclesiae; et per ipsam Legem inscriptam binis tabulis lapideis, et inclusam Arcae, significatus est Dominus quoad Verbum.

Nunc quia externa trahunt suam essentiam ab internis, et haec et illa ab intimo, quod ibi erat Lex, ideo sancta Verbi per omnia tabernaculi etiam repraesentata et significata sunt. Inde sequitur quod per ultima tabernaculi, quae erant aulaea et vela, ita tegumenta et continentia, significata sint ultima Verbi, quae sunt vera et bona sensus literae ejus. Quia illa significata sunt, ideo omnia aulaea et vela facta sunt ex xylino intertexto, et hyacinthino et purpura, et coccineo dibapho, cum cherubis, Exod.26:1,31,36. Quid per tabernaculum, et per omnia quae in illo erant, in genere et specie repraesentatum et significatum est, in **Arcanis Caelestibus** super illo capite Exodi explicatum est; et ibi ostensum quod per aulaea et vela repraesentata sint externa caeli et ecclesiae, ita quoque externa Verbi; tum quod per xylinum seu byssinum significatum sit verum ex origine spirituali, per hyacinthinum verum ex origine caelesti, per purpuram bonum caeleste, per coccineum dibaphum bonum spirituale, et per cherubos custodiae interiorum Verbi.

47 *Quod per externa templi Hierosolymitani repraesentata sint externa Verbi, quae sunt sensus literae ejus*, est quia simile per templum, quod per tabernaculum, repraesentatum est, nempe caelum et ecclesia, et inde quoque Verbum. Quod per templum Hierosolymitanum significatum sit Divinum Humanum Domini, docet Ipse apud Johannem,

Solvite templum hoc, et in tribus diebus exsuscitabo illud. Ipse loquebatur de templo corporis Sui. 2:19,21.

Et ubi intelligitur Dominus, etiam intelligitur Verbum, quia Dominus est Verbum. Nunc quia per interiora templi repraesentata sunt interiora caeli et ecclesiae, ita quoque Verbi, ideo per exteriora ejus repraesentata et significata sunt exteriora caeli et ecclesiae, ita quoque Verbi, quae sensus literae ejus sunt. De exterioribus templi legitur quod aedificata sint ex lapide integro, non caeso, et ex cedro intus, et quod omnes parietes ejus intus sculpti essent cherubis, palmis, et aperturis

of the presence on it – represented and so stood for the holy things of heaven and the church. The holy of holies, where the Ark of the Covenant was, represented and so stood for the inmost of heaven and the church. The Law itself inscribed upon two tables of stone and placed inside the Ark stood for the Lord in respect of the Word.

Now since outward aspects derive their essence from inward contents, and both of these derive theirs from the inmost, which in this case was the Law, therefore all the details of the tabernacle also represented and stood for the holy things of the Word. From this it follows that the outermost parts of the tabernacle – the curtains and veils, thus coverings and containers – meant the outermost form of the Word, which is the truths and forms of goodness belonging to its literal sense. It was because that was their meaning that all the curtains and veils were made of lawn interwoven, and violet and purple, and double-dyed red, with cherubim, Exod.26:1,31,36. What the tabernacle and all its contents represented and meant generally and specifically has been explained in **Arcana Caelestia**, in the commentary on that chapter of Exodus. There it was shown that the curtains and veils represented the outward aspects of heaven and the church, so also those of the Word; and that lawn or fine linen meant truth of a spiritual origin, violet truth of a celestial origin, purple celestial goodness, double-dyed red spiritual goodness, and the cherubim the protection of the inward contents of the Word.

47   *The outward features of the temple in Jerusalem represented the outward ones of the Word, that is, of its literal sense.* This is because the like was represented by the temple as by the tabernacle, namely heaven and the church, and so also the Word. The Lord Himself teaches in John that the temple in Jerusalem meant His Divine Human,

Break up this temple, and in three days I will raise it again. He was speaking about the temple of His body. 2:19,21.

When the Lord is meant, so also is the Word, for the Lord is the Word. Now since the more inward parts of the temple represented the more inward features of heaven and the church, and so those of the Word, therefore its more outward parts represented and stood for the outward features of heaven and the church, and so also those of the Word, that is, its literal sense. We read of the outward aspect of the temple, that it was built of whole, undressed stones, and inside of cedar wood; all its walls were carved inside with cherubim, palms,

florum, et quod solum obductum auro, 1 Reg.6:7,29,30, per quae omnia etiam significantur externa Verbi, quae sancta sensus literae ejus sunt.

48   *Quod Verbum in sua gloria per Dominum, cum transformatus est, repraesentatum sit.* De Domino coram Petro, Jacobo, et Johanne transformato legitur quod facies Ipsius fulserit sicut sol, vestimenta Ipsius facta sint sicut lux, et quod visi sint Moses et Elias cum Ipso colloquentes, et quod nubes lucida discipulos obtexerit et quod ex nube audita sit vox, dicens, Hic est Filius Meus dilectus; Ipsum audite, Matt.17:1-5. Instructus sum quod Dominus tunc repraesentaverit Verbum. Per faciem, quae fulsit sicut sol, repraesentatum est Divinum Bonum Ipsius; per vestimenta, quae facta sicut lux, Divinum Verum Ipsius; per Mosen et Eliam, Verbum Historicum et Propheticum – per Mosen Verbum quod per illum scriptum est, et in genere Verbum Historicum, ac per Eliam Verbum Propheticum; per nubem lucidam quae obtexit discipulos, Verbum in sensu literae; quare ex hac vox audita est, dicens Hic est Filius Meus dilectus; Ipsum audite. Omnia enim enuntiata et responsa e caelo, nusquam fiunt nisi per ultima qualia sunt in sensu literae Verbi, fiunt enim in pleno ex Domino.

49   Hactenus ostensum est quod Verbum in sensu naturali, qui est sensus literae, sit in suo sancto et in suo pleno; nunc aliquid dicetur quod Verbum in illo sensu etiam sit in sua **potentia**. Quanta et qualis est potentia Divini Veri in caelis, et quoque in terris, constare potest ex illis quae in opere **De Caelo et Inferno**, de potentia angelorum Caeli, n.228-233, dicta sunt. Potentia Divini Veri est imprimis contra falsa et mala, ita contra inferna; contra haec per vera ex sensu literae Verbi pugnandum est. Per vera apud hominem etiam est Domino potentia salvandi illum, nam homo per vera ex sensu literae Verbi reformatur et regeneratur, et tunc eximitur ex inferno et introducitur in caelum. Hanc potentiam suscepit Dominus etiam quoad Divinum Humanum Suum, postquam implevit omnia Verbi usque ad ultima ejus.

Quare Dominus ad principem sacerdotum dixit, quando reliqua per passionem crucis impleret,

---

1   quod *VR*: om *SS*
12 repraesentatum est *VR*: om *SS*
18 dicens *VR*: et dixit *SS*

and open flowers, and the floor was overlaid with gold, 1 Kings 6:7,29,30. All these things too stand for the outward aspects of the Word, which are the holy things in its literal sense.

48 *The Word in its glory was represented in the Lord at His transfiguration.* The description of the Lord's transfiguration in the presence of Peter, James, and John says that His face shone like the sun, His clothes became like light, and Moses and Elijah were seen speaking with Him, and that a shining cloud overshadowed the disciples, and a voice was heard from the cloud, saying, This is My beloved Son; listen to Him, Matt.17:1-5. I have been taught that the Lord then represented the Word. His face, which shone like the sun, represented His Divine Goodness; His clothes, which became like light, His Divine Truth. Moses and Elijah represented the historical and prophetic sections of the Word – Moses the part of the Word written by his instrumentality and the historical parts as a whole, Elijah the prophetic part. The shining cloud which overshadowed the disciples represented the Word in its literal sense; that is why a voice was heard from it saying, This is My beloved Son; listen to Him. For all statements and replies given from heaven are only given through the outermost forms, such as are in the literal sense of the Word; they acquire their fullness from the Lord.

49 Up to this point it has been shown that the Word in the natural, that is, literal sense is in its holiness and its fullness; now something must be said to show that the Word in that sense is also in its **power**. How great and what the nature are of Divine Truth in the heavens, and on earth too, becomes clear from what has been said in the work **Heaven and Hell**, §§228-233, about angels' power in heaven. The power of Divine Truth is directed in particular against falsities and evils, and so against the hells; truths drawn from the literal sense of the Word are needed to combat them. Also, it is in the truths residing in people that the Lord has the power to save them, for people are reformed and regenerated by means of truths derived from the literal sense of the Word. They are then rescued by Him from hell and brought into heaven. This power the Lord brought to His Divine Human also, after He had fulfilled all things in the Word right to the outermost level of it. This was why the Lord told the high priest, when through His passion on the cross He was about to accomplish those things He had still to fulfil, 2

Ex nunc videbitis Filium Hominis sedentem a dextris potentiae, venientem in nubibus caeli. Matt.26:64; Marc.14:62.

Filius Hominis est Dominus quoad Verbum, nubes caeli est Verbum in sensu literae, sedere a dextris Dei est omnipotentia per Verbum, ut quoque Marc.16:19. Potentia Domini ex ultimis veri repraesentata est per Naziraeos in Ecclesia Judaica; et per Simsonem, de quo dicitur quod Naziraeus esset ab utero matris, et quod potentia ejus constaret in crinibus ejus. Per Naziraeum et Naziraeatum etiam significatur crinis.

Quod potentia ejus in crinibus fuerit, manifestavit ipse, dicens,

Novacula non ascendit super caput meum, quia Naziraeus ego ab utero matris meae. Si radar, tunc recedet a me robur meum, et reddar infirmus, et ero sicut quivis homo. Jud.16:17.

Nemo scire potest cur Naziraeatus, per quem significatur crinis, institutus est, et unde est quod Simsoni fuerit robur ex crinibus, nisi sciat quid per caput in Verbo significatur. Per caput significatur sapientia caelestis, quae est angelis et hominibus a Domino per Divinum Verum; inde per crines capitis significatur sapientia caelestis in ultimis, et quoque Divinum Verum in ultimis.

Quia hoc per crines ex correspondentia cum caelis significabatur, ideo statutum pro Naziraeis erat, quod non raderent comam capitis sui, quia illa est Naziraeatus Dei super capite eorum, Num.6:1-21. Et quoque ideo statutum est quod summus sacerdos ac filii ejus non raderent caput suum, ne morerentur, et universa domus Israelis irasceretur, Lev.10:6. Quia crines propter illam significationem, quae est ex correspondentia, tam sancti erant, ideo Filius Hominis, qui est Dominus quoad Verbum, describitur etiam quoad crines, quod essent tanquam lana candida, tanquam nix, Apoc.1:14; similiter Antiquus Dierum, Dan.7:9. De hac re etiam videatur aliquid supra, n.35. In summa, quod potentia Divini Veri seu Verbi sit in sensu literae, est quia Verbum ibi est in suo pleno, et quia in illo sunt angeli utriusque regni Domini et homines simul.

13   radar SS^3, VR^3: rador SS^1, SS^2, VR^1, VR^2

Hereafter you will see the Son of Man seated at the right hand of power, coming on the clouds of heaven. Matt.26:64; Mark 14:62.

The Son of Man is the Lord in respect of the Word, the clouds of heaven are the Word in the literal sense, sitting at the right hand of God is almighty power exercised by means of the Word, as also in Mark 16:19. The Lord's power present in outermost forms of truth was represented by the Nazirites in the Jewish Church, and by Samson, of whom it is said that he was a Nazirite from his mother's womb and that his power lay in his hair. Furthermore hair is a sign of a Nazirite and Naziriteship. He himself showed that his power was in his hair when he said,

3

A razor has not gone up over my head, because I have been a Nazirite from my mother's womb. If I am shaved, then my strength will depart from me, and I shall become weak and be like any other person. Judg.16:17.

No one can know why Naziriteship, which the hair is a sign of, was established, or why Samson's strength came from his hair, unless they know the meaning of the head in the Word. The head stands for heavenly wisdom that angels and people obtain from the Lord through Divine Truth. Thus the hair on the head stands for heavenly wisdom at the outermost level, as well as Divine Truth at the outermost level.

It was because hair on account of its correspondence with the heavens had this meaning that Nazirites were required to refrain from shaving the hair on their head, for this is the Naziriteship of God on their head, Num.6:1-21. For the same reason it was a law that the high priest and his sons should not shave their head, lest they died and the whole house of Israel incurred anger, Lev.10:6. It was because the hair was so sacred, which was due to its correspondence, that the Son of Man, who is the Lord in respect of the Word, is also described as having hair like wool, white as snow, Rev.1:14, and so too the Ancient of Days, Dan.7:9. For something more about this, see §35 above. In short, the power of Divine Truth, or the Word, lies in its literal sense, because the Word is there in all its fullness, and this is the sense possessed alike by the angels of each of the Lord's kingdoms and by people.

4

5

Quod doctrina ecclesiae ex sensu literae Verbi haurienda sit, et per illum confirmanda

50 In praecedente articulo ostensum est quod Verbum in sensu literae sit in suo pleno, in suo sancto, et in sua potentia; et quia Dominus est Verbum, est enim omne Verbi, sequitur quod Dominus in illo sensu sit maxime praesens, et quod ex illo doceat et illustret hominem. Sed haec demonstranda sunt in hoc ordine –

i Quod Verbum absque doctrina non intelligatur
ii Quod doctrina e Verbi sensu literae haurienda sit
iii At quod Divinum Verum, quod doctrinae erit, non appareat aliis quam qui in illustratione a Domino sunt

51 i **Quod Verbum absque doctrina non intelligatur**, est quia Verbum in sensu literae ex meris correspondentiis consistit, ob finem ut spiritualia et caelestia inibi simul sint, ac unaquaevis vox illorum continens et fulcrum sit. Idcirco in sensu literae in quibusdam locis sunt non nuda vera sed vestita, quae vocantur apparentiae veri. Et sunt plura accommodata captui simplicium qui cogitationes non supra talia quae vident ante oculos, elevant; et aliqua quae apparent sicut contradictiones, cum tamen in Verbo in sua luce spectato nulla contradictio est. Et quoque in quibusdam locis apud Prophetas sunt nomina locorum et personarum collata, ex quibus non aliquis sensus potest elici, ut ex illis supra, n.15, allatis. Cum itaque Verbum in sensu literae tale est, constare potest quod non possit absque doctrina intelligi. Sed exempla hoc illustrent.

Dicitur quod Jehovam paeniteat, Exod.32:12,14; Jon.3:9; 4:2, dicitur etiam quod Jehovam non paeniteat, Num.23:19; 1 Sam.15:29. Haec absque doctrina non conformantur.

The teaching of the church is to be drawn from the literal sense of the Word and supported by it

50   It was shown in the previous section that the Word is in its fullness, holiness, and power in the literal sense. Since the Lord is the Word – for it is He that constitutes the Word, all of it – it follows that the Lord is most especially present in that sense and by means of it teaches and enlightens a person. But these points must be shown to be so in the following order –

i   The Word cannot be understood without teaching
ii   This teaching is to be drawn from the literal sense of the Word
iii   But Divine Truth, which is the substance of teaching, is not visible to any but those who are enlightened by the Lord

51   i **The Word cannot be understood without teaching.** This is because the Word in its literal sense is composed of pure correspondences, to the end that spiritual and celestial things may be simultaneously there within it; every single expression serves to contain and support them. This is why certain places in the literal sense do not contain bare truths but those which are clothed and are called appearances of truth. Many truths are presented in a way suited to the understanding of simple people whose thoughts are limited to the kinds of things they see before their eyes. Sometimes they look like contradictions, but in fact no contradictions exist in the Word when viewed in its own light. Also in certain places among the Prophets there are collections of the names of places and persons from which no meaning can be gleaned, such as those quoted above, in §15. All this being what the Word is like in the literal sense it is perfectly clear that it cannot be understood without teaching. But let examples help to illustrate this.

2   It says that Jehovah relents, at Exod.32:12,14; Jon.3:9; 4:2, and also that Jehovah does not relent, at Num.23:19; 1 Sam.15:29. These statements cannot be reconciled without that teaching.

Dicitur quod Jehovah visitet iniquitatem patrum super filios ad tertiam et quartam generationem, Num.14:18, ac dicitur quod non morietur pater propter filium, nec filius propter patrem, sed quisque in peccato suo, Deut.24:16. Haec non discordant sed concordant per doctrinam.

Dicit Jesus,

Petite et dabitur vobis, quaerite et invenietis, pulsate et aperietur vobis. Quisquis petit, accipiet, et quaerit, inveniet, et pulsanti aperietur. Matt.7:7,8; 21:21,22.

Absque doctrina crederetur quod quisque accepturus sit quod petit, sed ex doctrina creditur quod quicquid homo petit non ex se sed ex Domino, hoc detur; hoc enim Dominus etiam docet,

Si manseritis in Me et verba Mea in vobis manserint, quicquid volueritis, petetis, et fiet vobis. Joh.15:7.

Dicit Dominus,

Beati pauperes, quoniam illorum est regnum Dei. Luc.6:20.

Absque doctrina cogitari potest quod pauperibus sit caelum et non divitibus, sed doctrina docet quod pauperes spiritu intelligantur, nam dicit Dominus,

Beati pauperes spiritu, quia eorum est regnum caelorum. Matt.5:3.

Dicit Dominus,

Ne judicate ne judicemini. Cum quo judicio judicatis, judicabimini. Matt.7:1,2; Luc.6:37.

Hoc absque doctrina potest adduci ad confirmandum quod non dicendum sit de malo quod sit malum, ita non judicandum quod malus sit malus. Sed ex doctrina licet judicare, at juste, dicit enim Dominus,

Justum judicium judicate. Joh.7:24.

---

8 et quaerit SS^1: et [qui] quaerit SS^2, SS^3
14 petetis SS^2, SS^3: petitis SS^1; petite VR

It says that Jehovah visits the wickedness of the fathers upon the sons to the third and fourth generation, at Num.14:18, and it says that a father shall not die on account of his son, nor a son on account of his father, but each in his own sin, at Deut.24:16. Teaching can show that these statements do not conflict but are in harmony.

Jesus says, 3

Ask and it will be given to you, seek and you will find, knock and it will be opened to you. Whoever asks will receive, and one who seeks will find, and to one who knocks it will be opened. Matt.7:7,8; 21:21,22.

Without teaching people might suppose that all receive what they ask for, but with that teaching they can see that whatever a person asks not for a selfish reason but for the Lord's sake, that is granted; for this the Lord also teaches,

If you remain in Me and My words remain in you, you will ask whatever you will, and it will be done for you. John 15:7.

The Lord says, 4

Blessed are the poor, for theirs is the kingdom of God. Luke 6:20.

Without teaching people might think that heaven was for the poor and not the rich, but that teaching shows that the poor in spirit are meant, for the Lord says,

Blessed are the poor in spirit, for theirs is the kingdom of the heavens. Matt.5:3.

The Lord says, 5

Do not judge, so that you are not judged. With whatever judgment you judge, so will you be judged. Matt.7:1,2; Luke 6:37.

Without teaching this statement could be used to support the idea that what is evil must not be declared to be such, thus a person who is wicked must not be judged to be so. But that teaching does allow judgment to be passed, so long as it is done justly, for the Lord says,

Give just judgments. John 7:24.

Jesus dicit,

Nolite vocari doctor, quia unus est doctor vester, Christus. Ne vocetis patrem vestrum in terra, unus namque est Pater vester in caelis. Nec vocemini magistri, unus enim est vester magister, Christus.
5 Matt.23:8-10.

Absque doctrina foret quod non liceat vocare aliquem doctorem, patrem, et magistrum, sed ex doctrina scitur quod liceat in naturali sensu, at non in spirituali.
Jesus dixit ad discipulos,

10 Quando sedebit Filius Hominis super throno gloriae Suae, sedebitis etiam vos super duodecim thronis judicantes duodecim tribus Israelis. Matt.19:28.

Ex his verbis concludi potest quod etiam discipuli Domini judicaturi sint, cum tamen neminem judicare possunt. Doctrina
15 itaque revelabit hoc arcanum per hoc, quod solus Dominus, qui est omniscius et novit omnium corda, judicaturus sit et judicare possit, et quod per duodecim discipulos Ipsius, intelligatur ecclesia quoad omnia vera et bona, quae ei sunt a Domino per Verbum. Ex quo doctrina concludit quod illa
20 judicatura sint unumquemvis, secundum Domini verba apud Johannem 3:17,18; 12:47,48.

Qui absque doctrina legit Verbum, non scit quomodo cohaerent illa quae de gente Judaica et de Hierosolyma apud Prophetas dicuntur, quod ecclesia apud illam gentem, et sedes
25 ejus in illa urbe, in aeternum mansura sit, ut in sequentibus –

Visitabit Jehovah gregem Suum, domum Jehudae, et ponet illos sicut equum gloriae in bello. Ex Illo angularis, ex Illo clavus, et ex Illo arcus belli. Sach.10:3,4,6,7.
Ecce Ego venio, ut habitem in medio tui. Et Jehovah haereditatem
30 faciet Jehudam, et eliget rursus Hierosolymam. Sach.2:14-16.
Fiet in die illo, montes stillabunt mustum, et colles fluent lacte. Et Jehudah in aeternum erit, et Hierosolyma in generationem et generationem. Joel.4:18-20.
Ecce dies venientes, quibus seminabo domum Israelis et domum
35 Jehudae semine hominis; et quibus pangam cum domo Israelis

2   Ne *VR*: Nec *SS*

Jesus says, 6

Do not have yourselves called teacher, for you have one teacher, Christ. Do not call anyone on earth your father, for you have one Father in the heavens. And do not have yourselves called master, for you have one master, Christ. Matt.23:8-10.

Without teaching this would mean that none is allowed to call anyone teacher, father, or master; but teaching shows that it is allowable to do so in the natural sense but not the spiritual.

Jesus said to the disciples, 7

When the Son of Man sits on the throne of His glory, you too will sit on twelve thrones judging the twelve tribes of Israel. Matt.19:28.

It might be inferred from these words that the Lord's disciples too are to act as judges, though in fact they can judge no one. Teaching therefore will reveal the mystery by the fact that the Lord alone, who is omniscient and knows the hearts of all, can and will be judge. His twelve disciples mean the church in respect of all its truths and all its kinds of goodness, which the Lord imparts to it by means of the Word. Teaching infers from this that it is the truths and forms of goodness which will judge everyone, as accords with the Lord's words in John 3:17,18; 12:47,48.

Those who read the Word without teaching do not know 8 how things said in the Prophets about the Jewish nation and about Jerusalem square with one another. The Prophets say that the church among that nation and its settlement in that city will last for ever, in the following places for example –

Jehovah will visit His flock, the house of Judah, and will place them as a glorious horse in battle. From Him comes the cornerstone, from Him the tent peg, from Him the battle bow. Zech.10:3,4,6,7.
Behold, I am coming in order to dwell in your midst. And Jehovah will inherit Judah, and will again choose Jerusalem. Zech.2:10-12.
It will happen on that day, that the mountains will drip new wine, and the hills will flow with milk. And Judah will exist for ever, and Jerusalem from generation to generation. Joel 3:18-20.
Behold, the days are coming in which I will sow the house of Israel and the house of Judah with the seed of human beings, and in which I will

et cum domo Jehudae faedus novum. Et hoc faedus; dabo legem Meam in medio eorum, et super cor eorum scribam illam, et ero illis in Deum, et illi erunt Mihi in populum. Jer.31:27,31,33. In die illo apprehendent decem viri ex omnibus linguis gentium, alam viri Judaei, dicentes, Ibimus vobiscum, quia audivimus Deum vobiscum. Sach.8:22,23.

Similiter alibi, ut Esai.44:24,26; 49:22,23; 65:9; 66:20,22; Jer.3:18; 23:5; 50:1,19,20; Nahum 2:1; Mal.3:4 – in quibus locis agitur de adventu Domini, et quod hoc tunc futurum sit.

Contrarium autem in pluribus aliis locis dicitur, ex quibus hic modo adducetur –

Occultabo facies Meas ab illis; videbo quid posteritas illorum, generatio enim perversionum illi, filii in quibus fidelitas non. Dixerim, In extremos angulos ejiciam illos, cessare faciam ab homine memoriam illorum. Nam gens deperdita consiliis illi, nec in illis intelligentia. De vite Sodomae vitis eorum et de agris Gomorrhae; uvae ejus uvae fellis; botri amaritudinum illis. Venenum draconum vinum illorum, et fel aspidum crudele. Nonne illud absconditum apud Me, obsignatum in thesauris Meis? Mihi vindicta et retributio. Deut.32:20-35.

Haec de illa gente dicta sunt. Et similia alibi, ut Esai.3:1,2,8; 5:3-6; Deut.9:5,6; Matt.12:39; 23:27,28; Joh.8:44; et ubivis apud Jeremiam et Ezechielem. Sed haec, quae apparent contrarientia, patebunt ut concordantia ex doctrina, quae docet quod per Israelem et per Jehudam in Verbo non intelligantur Israel et Jehudah sed ecclesia in utroque sensu, in uno quod devastata sit, in altero quod a Domino instauranda.

His similia sunt alia in Verbo, ex quibus manifeste patet quod Verbum absque doctrina non intelligatur.

52 Ex his constare potest quod qui Verbum absque doctrina legunt, aut qui non ex Verbo sibi doctrinam comparant, sint in obscuro de omni veritate, et quod mens eorum sit vaga et incerta, prona in errores, et quoque facilis ad haereses, quas etiam amplectuntur si favor aut auctoritas aspirat et fama

---

15 consiliis SS^3: consilii SS^1, SS^2
18 Nonne SS^3: Omne SS^1, SS^2

make with the house of Israel and the house of Judah a new covenant. And this is the covenant: I will put My law in the midst of them, and will write it on their heart, and I will be their God, and they will be My people. Jer.31:27,31,33.
On that day ten men from every language of the nations will take hold of the hem of a man of Judah, saying, We will go with you, for we have heard that God is with you. Zech.8:22,23.

Statements like these occur in other places, such as Isa.44:24,26; 49:22,23; 65:9; 66:20,22; Jer.3:18; 23:5; 50:1,19,20; Nahum 1:15; Mal.3:4. In all of these places the subject is the coming of the Lord and what will happen at that time.

But what is stated in very many other places runs counter to this, just one of which places will be quoted here – 9

I will conceal My face from them; I will see what their future will be, for they are a perverse generation, sons in whom there is no faithfulness. I would have said, I will expel them to the remotest corners, I will make the memory of them cease from humankind. For they are a nation from whom counsel has perished, nor is there intelligence in them. From the vine of Sodom comes their vine, and from the fields of Gomorrah; their grapes are grapes of poison, they have clusters of bitterness. The poison of snakes is their wine, and the cruel poison of asps. Is not this hidden away with Me, sealed up in My treasures? Vengeance is Mine, and recompense. Deut.32:20-35.

The words quoted here refer to that nation, and there are others like them elsewhere, for instance at Isa.3:1,2,8; 5:3-6; Deut.9:5,6; Matt.12:39; 23:27,28; John 8:44; and all through Jeremiah and Ezekiel. Yet these statements, which seem to run counter, will be shown by teaching to be in fact in keeping; that teaching shows that in the Word Israel and Judah serve to mean not Israel and Judah but the church, in two senses – in one sense that it has been laid waste, in the other that it is to be raised up by the Lord.

There are further places like these in the Word, which show plainly that the Word cannot be understood without teaching.

52 These facts make it clear that those who read the Word without teaching, or who do not acquire such teaching for themselves from the Word, are in the dark as regards every truth. Their minds are vacillating and uncertain, prone to errors and easily led into heresies, and indeed they embrace these if they have the slightest

non periclitatur. Est enim Verbum illis sicut candelabrum absque lumine, ac vident in umbra tanquam multa, et tamen vident vix aliquid, nam sola doctrina est lucerna. Vidi tales exploratos ab angelis, ac inventos quod confirmare possent ex Verbo quodcunque volunt, et quod confirment quae sunt amoris sui, et amoris illorum quibus favent. Et vidi illos nudatos vestibus, signum quod essent absque veris. Vestes ibi sunt vera.

53   ii **Quod doctrina ex sensu literae Verbi haurienda sit, et confirmanda**, est quia Dominus ibi et non alibi apud hominem, praesens est, ac illustrat et docet illum vera ecclesiae; et Dominus nusquam operatur aliquid nisi in pleno, et Verbum in sensu literae est in suo pleno, ut supra ostensum est. Inde est quod doctrina ex sensu literae haurienda sit.

54   Quod Verbum per doctrinam non modo intelligatur sed etiam quasi luceat, est quia Verbum absque doctrina non intelligitur et est sicut candelabrum absque lumine, ut supra ostensum est; ideo Verbum per doctrinam intelligitur et est sicut candelabrum cum accenso lumine. Homo tunc videt plura quam prius viderat, et quoque intelligit illa quae non prius intellexerat; obscura et discordantia vel non videt et praeterit vel videt et explicat ut cum doctrina concordent. Quod Verbum ex doctrina videatur, et quoque secundum illam explicetur, testatur experientia in Christiano orbe. Omnes Reformati enim vident Verbum ex sua doctrina, et Verbum secundum illam explicant, similiter Pontificii ex sua et secundum illam; imo Judaei ex sua et secundum illam, consequenter falsa ex doctrina falsa, et vera ex doctrina vera. Inde patet quod doctrina vera sit instar lucernae in tenebris ac instar indicis in viis.

At doctrina non modo ex sensu literae Verbi haurienda est sed etiam per illum confirmanda, nam si non per illum confirmatur, apparet verum doctrinae sicut modo intelligentia hominis foret in illa, et non Divina Sapientia Domini, et sic foret doctrina sicut domus in aere et non super terra, ita non fundata.

popularity or authoritative support, and provided there is no risk to their own reputation. For them the Word is like a lampstand without any lights, and in the dim light they think they see much, when in fact they can see hardly anything, since it is only teaching that is a source of light. I have witnessed such people being tested by angels, who found that they could prove from the Word anything they wished; and what they proved was what arose from their self-love or the love of those whom they favour. But I saw them stripped of their clothes, a sign that they were devoid of truths; clothing in that world consists of truths.

53 ii **Teaching is to be drawn from the literal sense of the Word, and corroborated by means of it.** This is because the Lord is present with people in that sense and nowhere else, enlightening them and teaching them the truths of the church. The Lord never performs any act except in fullness, and the Word is in its fullness in the literal sense, as was shown above. This is why teaching is to be drawn from the literal sense.

54 The reason why the Word is not only made intelligible by teaching but also spreads light, so to speak, is that without teaching the Word cannot be understood and is like a lampstand without a light, as shown above. So the Word is made intelligible by teaching and resembles a lampstand with a light that has been lit. Then people see more than they had seen before and understand too things they had not previously understood. What is obscure and in disagreement they either fail to see and pass over, or they do see and explain them so that they are in harmony with the teaching. Proof that people view the Word in the light of teaching and also explain it in accordance with that teaching may be gained from experience in the Christian world. For all the Reformed view the Word in the light of their teaching, and this determines how they explain it; likewise the Roman Catholics view it in the light of their teaching, and their explanation is determined by this. Even the Jews view it in the light of their teaching, and their explanation is determined by this. Thus false ideas result from false teaching, and true ideas from true teaching. From this it is evident that true teaching is like a lamp shining in the darkness, and like a signpost on a road.

Teaching however must not only be drawn from the literal sense of the Word but also corroborated by means of it. If it is not corroborated by it the truth which that teaching presents would appear to have only human discernment, not the Lord's Divine Wisdom, within it, and so the teaching would be like a house up in the air, not down on the ground, thus lacking any foundations.

55 Doctrina genuini veri ex sensu literali Verbi etiam plene potest hauriri, nam Verbum in illo sensu est tanquam homo vestitus, cui facies est nuda et quoque manus sunt nudae. Omnia quae ad vitam hominis, ita quae ad salutem ejus, pertinent sunt ibi nuda, reliqua autem vestita, et in multis locis ubi vestita sunt transparent, sicut facies per tenue sericum. Etiam vera Verbi, sicut multiplicantur ex amore illorum et sicut per hunc ordinantur, ita clarius et clarius per vestes pellucent et apparent. Sed hoc quoque per doctrinam.

56 Credi potest quod doctrina genuini veri comparari possit per sensum spiritualem Verbi qui datur per scientiam correspondentiarum; at doctrina per illum non comparatur sed modo illustratur et corroboratur, nam – ut prius, n.26, dictum est – in sensum spiritualem Verbi per correspondentias nemo venit nisi prius in genuinis veris ex doctrina sit. Si non in genuinis veris prius est, potest homo Verbum per aliquot correspondentias notas falsificare, conjungendo et explicando illas ad confirmandum id quod menti ex principio capto inhaeret. Praeterea, sensus spiritualis non datur alicui nisi a solo Domino, et custoditur ab Ipso sicut custoditur caelum, nam caelum est in illo. Praestat itaque ut homo studeat Verbo in sensu literae; ex illo solo datur doctrina.

57 iii **Quod genuinum verum quod doctrinae erit, in sensu literae Verbi non appareat aliis quam qui in illustratione sunt a Domino.** Illustratio est a solo Domino, et apud illos qui amant vera quia vera sunt, et faciunt illa usus vitae; apud alios non datur illustratio in Verbo. Quod illustratio sit a solo Domino, est quia Dominus est in omnibus Verbi. Quod illustratio sit apud illos qui amant vera quia vera sunt, et faciunt illa usus vitae, est quia illi sunt in Domino et Dominus in illis. Est enim Dominus Divinum Suum Verum; hoc cum amatur quia Divinum Verum est, et hoc amatur quando fit usus, tunc Dominus in illo est apud hominem. Haec etiam Dominus docet apud Johannem,

In die illo cognoscetis quod vos in Me et Ego in vobis. Qui habet praecepta Mea et facit illa, ille amat Me, et Ego amabo illum et manifestabo illi Me Ipsum. Et ad illum veniam et mansionem apud illum faciam. 14:20,21,23.

55   Teaching containing genuine truth can even fully be drawn from the literal sense of the Word, for the Word in that sense resembles a person wearing clothes, but whose face and hands are bare. Everything needed for people's life, and so everything needed for their salvation, is uncovered there, though the remainder is clothed. In many places where it is clothed it still shines through, like a face with a thin veil over it. Furthermore, as the truths of the Word increase in number, because they are loved and this love gives them shape, so they show through their clothing and become visible more and more clearly. But teaching too enables them to do so.

56   It might be thought that teaching containing genuine truth could be acquired by means of the spiritual sense of the Word, which is granted through knowledge of correspondences. But such teaching is not acquired by means of that sense, only illustrated and supported by it, for – as was said previously, at §26 – no one arrives at the spiritual sense of the Word by means of correspondences unless they are first of all in possession of genuine truths obtained from teaching. If they are not first of all in possession of genuine truths people who know a few correspondences can falsify the Word by combining and interpreting them so as to support what is rooted in their mind as a result of their adopting some fundamental tenet. What is more, the spiritual sense is not granted to anyone except by the Lord alone, and it is guarded by Him just as heaven is guarded, for heaven is in possession of that sense. Better for people therefore to apply themselves to the Word in the literal sense; this alone is the source that provides teaching.

57   iii **Genuine truth, on which teaching must be based, is not visible in the literal sense of the Word to any but those who are enlightened by the Lord.** Enlightenment comes only from the Lord, and to those who love truths for truths' sake and make these their guide to a useful life. No others find enlightenment in the Word. Enlightenment comes only from the Lord because the Lord is there in every detail of the Word. And the reason why it comes to those who love truths for truths' sake and make these their guide to a useful life, is that they are in the Lord and the Lord is in them. For the Lord is His own Divine Truth; when this is loved for Divine Truth's sake, and this is loved when it passes into useful deeds, then the Lord is present with a person in it. The Lord, moreover, teaches these things in John,

On that day you will know that you are in Me and I in you. Those who have My commandments and keep them love Me, and I shall love them and show Myself to them. And I shall come to them and make My dwelling with them. 14:20,21,23.

Et apud Matthaeum,

Beati mundi corde, quia hi Deum videbunt. 5:8.

Hi sunt qui in illustratione sunt cum legunt Verbum et apud quos Verbum lucet et translucet.

58 Quod Verbum apud illos luceat et transluceat, est quia singulis Verbi sensus spiritualis et caelestis inest, et hi sensus sunt in luce caeli, quare Dominus per illos sensus et per illorum lucem influit in sensum naturalem et in hujus lucem apud hominem. Inde homo ex interiore perceptione agnoscit verum, et dein in cogitatione sua videt illud, et hoc quoties in affectione veri propter verum est, ex affectione enim venit perceptio, ex perceptione cogitatio, et sic fit agnitio, quae fides vocatur. Sed de hac re plura dicentur in sequente articulo de conjunctione Domini cum homine per Verbum.

59 Apud hos primum est quod ex Verbi sensu literali comparent sibi doctrinam; ita accendunt sibi lucernam ad ulteriorem progressum. Postquam autem comparata est doctrina et sic accensa lucerna, ex illa vident Verbum. Illi autem qui non comparant sibi doctrinam, primum inquirunt num doctrina ab aliis data, et a communi coetu recepta, cum Verbo concordet; et ad illa quae concordant consentiunt, et ad illa quae non concordant dissentiunt. Ita fit illis sua doctrina et per doctrinam sua fides. Sed hoc fit solum apud illos qui non distracti a negotiis mundi possunt videre; hi, si amant vera quia vera sunt et faciunt illa usus vitae, in illustratione sunt a Domino. Reliqui qui in aliqua vita sunt secundum vera, possunt ab illis discere.

60 Contrarium fit illis qui ex doctrina religionis falsae legunt Verbum, et plus illis qui doctrinam illam ex Verbo confirmant et tunc spectant ad sui gloriam aut ad mundi opes. Apud hos verum Verbi est sicut in umbra noctis et falsum sicut in luce diei; legunt verum sed non vident illud, et si umbram ejus vident, falsificant illud. Sunt hi de quibus Dominus dicit quod oculos habeant et non videant, et quod aures et non intelligant, Matt.13:14,15. Nam nihil aliud occaecat hominem quam proprium ejus et confirmatio falsi. Proprium hominis est amor sui et inde fastus propriae intelligentiae, ac confirmatio

And in Matthew,

Blessed are the pure in heart, for they will see God. 5:8.

Those are meant who are enlightened when they read the Word, and for whom the Word shines and shows through.

58 The reason why for them the Word shines and shows through is that the details of the Word contain a spiritual and a celestial sense, and these senses are filled with the light of heaven. Therefore the Lord by means of those senses and their light floods into the natural sense, and into the light this sheds on people. So it is that people acknowledge truth by an inner perception, and then see it in their thought processes; this happens whenever they have affection for truth for truth's sake. For the affection leads to perception, the perception to thought, and thus comes the acknowledgement, which is called faith. But more will be said about this in the next section, where the Lord's link with people by means of the Word is the subject.

59 In the case of these people they first of all go for themselves to the literal sense of the Word to acquire teaching from it; and by doing so they light a lamp for themselves which enables them to go further. Once they have acquired the teaching however and so the lamp has been lit they see the Word in the light of that teaching. But those who do not acquire teaching for themselves first of all ask whether the teaching provided by others and commonly accepted is in harmony with the Word; and they go along with aspects of it that are in harmony, and reject those that are not. Thus what they go along with of such teaching becomes theirs, and this comes to be what they believe. Yet this happens only in the case of those who are not distracted by worldly affairs and are free to see such things. If these people love truths for truths' own sake and are putting them to use in life they are receiving enlightenment from the Lord. The rest leading some kind of life in accord with truths are able to learn from them.

60 The reverse happens with those who follow the teaching provided by a false religion in their reading of the Word, and the more so in the case of those who use the Word to substantiate that teaching, having in view then their own glory or worldly wealth. With these people the truth of the Word is as if plunged in the shades of night, while falsity is as if in daylight. They read what is true yet do not see it, or if they do see a shadow of it they falsify it. They are those of whom the Lord says they have eyes and do not see, and have ears and do not understand, Matt.13:14,15. For nothing else makes people blind but the self within them and their substantiation

falsi est caligo mentiens lucem. Lux horum est mere naturalis, et visus illorum est sicut videntis larvas in umbra.

61 Datum est loqui cum multis post mortem qui crediderunt se sicut stellae lucituros in caelo, quia, ut dixerunt, sanctum habuerunt Verbum, saepius perlegerunt illud, plura inde collegerunt, per quae fidei suae dogmata confirmaverunt, et per id in mundo ut docti celebrati sunt, ex quo credebant se Michaeles et Raphaeles futuros. Sed plures ex illis explorati sunt, ex quo amore studuerunt Verbo, ac inventi quod aliqui ex amore sui ut magni in mundo apparerent, et sicut primates ecclesiae colerentur, aliqui autem ex amore mundi ut lucrarentur opes. Hi dum explorati sunt quid scirent ex Verbo, compertum est quod inde nihil genuini veri scirent sed modo tale quod vocatur verum falsificatum, quod in se est falsum. Et dictum est illis quod hoc illis esset ex causa quia ipsi et mundus fuerunt fines seu, quod idem est, amores, et non Dominus et caelum; et cum ipsi et mundus sunt fines, tunc cum legunt Verbum, haeret mens illorum in seipsis et in mundo, et inde cogitant jugiter ex suo proprio, quod in caligine est quoad omnia quae caeli sunt, in quo statu non potest homo a Domino subduci ex proprio et sic elevari in lucem caeli, proinde nec aliquem influxum a Domino per caelum recipere.

Vidi etiam hos in caelum admissos, at cum ibi inventi sunt quod absque veris essent, dejecti sunt; sed usque remansit apud illos fastus quod meruerint. Aliter factum est cum illis qui studuerunt Verbo ex affectione sciendi verum quia est verum et quia inservit usibus vitae, non modo suae sed etiam proximi. Illos vidi elevatos in caelum et sic in lucem in qua est Divinum Verum ibi, et simul tunc exaltatos in sapientiam angelicam, et in felicitatem ejus, quae est vita aeterna.

of what is false. The self within a person consists of self-love and consequent arrogance of self-intelligence, and the substantiation of what is false is thick darkness presenting itself as light. The light these people have is wholly natural, and their vision is like that of someone seeing ghostly figures in the dark.

61 I have been permitted to talk to many after their death who believed they would shine like stars in heaven. For, so they said, they regarded the Word as holy, frequently read it right through, collected many passages from it to support the dogmas of the faith they adhere to, and by means of all this in the world gained a reputation for being learned. As a result they thought they would be like Michael and Raphael.

2 Many of these however were questioned to see what love had impelled them to study the Word. Some, it was discovered, had been impelled by self-love, wishing to appear in the world to be great, and to be revered in the way the leaders of the church are, and some were impelled by worldly love, hoping thereby to become wealthy. When they went on to be questioned to see what they had learned from the Word it proved that they had learned no genuine truth from it, only the sort called falsified truth, which in fact is falsity through and through. They were told that the reason this happened to them was that the ends they had in view – or what amount to the same thing, their loves – were self and the world, not the Lord and heaven. And if people's ends in view are self and the world, then when they read the Word their minds do not rise above self and the world, and their thinking is constantly dominated by their self-centredness, which is enveloped in thick darkness in all they think about heaven. In that state people cannot be drawn away by the Lord from their concentration on self and so lifted up into the light of heaven, and consequently cannot receive any influence from the Lord through heaven.

3 I have also seen these people allowed into heaven, but when it was discovered there that they were devoid of truths they were thrown out. Yet they still retained their proud conviction that they deserved admission. Quite different was the treatment of those whose study of the Word had been impelled by a desire to know the truth because it is true and because it serves to promote a useful life, not only their own but their neighbour's too. These I saw lifted up to heaven, to enjoy the light which there surrounds Divine Truth, and at the same time they were raised to a state of angelic wisdom and the happiness this brings, that is, eternal life.

Quod per sensum literae Verbi sit conjunctio cum Domino et consociatio cum angelis

62 Quod per Verbum sit conjunctio cum Domino, est quia Verbum de solo Ipso agit, et per id Dominus est omne in omnibus ejus, et vocatur Verbum, ut in **Doctrina de Domino** ostensum est. Quod in sensu literae sit conjunctio, est quia Verbum in illo sensu est in suo pleno, in suo sancto, et in sua potentia, ut supra in suo articulo ostensum est. Conjunctio non apparet homini, sed est in affectione veri et in perceptione ejus, ita in Divini Veri amore et fide apud illum.

63 Quod per sensum literae sit consociatio cum angelis caeli, est quia illi sensui inest sensus spiritualis et sensus caelestis, et in his sensibus sunt angeli – angeli regni spiritualis in sensu spirituali Verbi, et angeli regni caelestis in sensu caelesti ejus. Hi sensus evolvuntur ex sensu naturali Verbi, qui est sensus literae, dum homo verus in illo est. Evolutio est instantanea, proinde etiam consociatio.

64 Quod angeli spirituales in sensu spirituali Verbi sint et angeli caelestes in sensu caelesti ejus, manifestatum est mihi per multam experientiam. Datum est percipere quod cum legi Verbum in sensu literae ejus, communicatio facta sit cum caelis, nunc cum hac illorum societate, nunc cum illa, et quod ea quae ego secundum sensum naturalem intellexi, angeli spirituales secundum sensum spiritualem et angeli caelestes secundum sensum caelestem intellexerint, et hoc in instanti. Haec communicatio quia per aliquot millenas vices percepta est, de illa non relicta est mihi ulla dubitatio. Sunt etiam spiritus qui infra caelos sunt, et hac communicatione abutuntur, recitant enim aliquot dicta ex sensu literae Verbi, et illico animadvertunt et notant societatem cum qua communicatio fit. Hoc etiam saepe vidi et audivi. Ex his per vivam experientiam datum est scire quod Verbum quoad sensum literae ejus sit Divinum

The literal sense of the Word produces a link with the Lord and association with the angels

62   The Word produces a link with the Lord, because the Word has Him alone as its subject, causing the Lord to be its all in all and to be called the Word, as has been shown in **Teaching concerning the Lord**. The link resides in the literal sense because in that sense the Word is in its fullness, holiness, and power, as shown above in the section on this subject. The link is not visible to people but lies in their affection for and perception of truth, and so in their love of and belief in Divine Truth.

63   The reason why the literal sense produces association with the angels in heaven is that the spiritual and celestial senses are contained in it, and these are the senses that the angels possess – the angels of the spiritual kingdom the spiritual sense of the Word, and the angels of the celestial kingdom its celestial sense. These senses are unwound from the natural sense of the Word, that is, the literal sense, when a person who is sincere is attentive to this sense. The unwinding takes place instantly, and so therefore does the association.

64   It has been made evident to me by long experience that spiritual angels possess the spiritual sense of the Word and celestial angels its celestial sense. I have been allowed to perceive that when I read the Word in its literal sense communication was established with the heavens, at one time with one community there, at another time with another, and that the things which I understood according to the natural sense were understood by spiritual angels according to the spiritual sense, and by celestial angels according to the celestial sense, and in an instant. Since I have perceived this communication some thousands of times I have no doubt left concerning it. There are also spirits below the heavens who misuse this communication, for they repeat some verses from the literal sense of the Word and immediately notice and mark down the community with which communication is established. This too I have seen and heard many times. These direct experiences have enabled me to know that the Word in its literal sense

medium conjunctionis cum Domino et cum caelo. De hac conjunctione per Verbum videantur etiam quae in opere **De Caelo et Inferno**, n.303-310, allata sunt.

65 Sed quomodo evolutio illorum sensuum fit, etiam paucis dicetur. Sed ut intelligatur, recolligenda sunt quae supra, n.6,38, de ordine successivo et de ordine simultaneo dicta sunt, nempe quod caeleste, spirituale, et naturale sequantur in ordine successivo unum post alterum a supremis quae in caelo sunt ad ultima quae in mundo; et quod eadem in ordine simultaneo sint in ultimo, quod est naturale, unum juxta alterum ab intimis ad extima; et quod similiter sint successivi sensus Verbi, caelestis et spiritualis, simul in naturali. His comprehensis aliquantum explicari ad intellectum potest quomodo bini sensus, spiritualis et caelestis, evolvuntur ex sensu naturali, quando homo Verbum legit, tunc enim angelus spiritualis evocat spirituale, et angelus caelestis evocat caeleste. Nec aliter possunt, sunt enim homogenea, ac naturae et essentiae illorum consentanea.

66 Sed hoc primum illustretur per comparationes ex tribus regnis naturae, quae vocantur animale, vegetabile, et minerale.

Ex regno animali. Ex cibo, cum factus est chylus, hauriunt et evocant vasa suum sanguinem, fibrae nerveae suum succum, et substantiae, quae sunt origines fibrarum, suum spiritum animalem.

Ex regno vegetabili. Arbor cum trunco, ramis, foliis, et fructibus stat super radice sua, et ex humo per radicem extrahit et evocat succum crassiorem pro trunco, ramis, et foliis, puriorem pro carne fructuum, et purissimum pro seminibus intra fructus.

Ex regno minerali. In gremio terrae in quibusdam locis sunt minerae impregnatae auro, argento, et ferro; ex halitibus in terra reconditis trahit aurum suum elementum, argentum suum, et ferrum suum.

67 Illustretur nunc per exemplum quomodo angeli spirituales extrahunt suum sensum, et angeli caelestes suum, ex sensu naturali, in quo est Verbum apud homines. In exemplum sint quinque praecepta decalogi.

---

5   recolligenda sunt quae *SS³*: recolligendum est quod *SS¹*, *SS²*
32 et ferro *SS*: cupro et ferro *VR*

is a Divine means of being linked with the Lord and with heaven. Regarding this link by means of the Word see also what has been presented in the work **Heaven and Hell**, §§303-310.

65 But a brief explanation showing how those inner senses are unwound must also be given. To make it intelligible however it is necessary to recall what was stated above, at §§6,38, about successive order and simultaneous order. That is, celestial, spiritual, and natural follow in successive order one after the other, from highest things in heaven to lowest in the world; and the same all exist in simultaneous order at the lowest level, that is, in what is natural, one alongside another from those which are inmost to those that are outermost. And in a similar way the successive senses of the Word, the celestial and the spiritual, are simultaneously present in the natural. Once these ideas have been grasped it is possible to provide some intelligible explanation of how both senses, the spiritual and the celestial, are unwound from the natural sense when a person is reading the Word; for when a person does so a spiritual angel elicits what is spiritual from it and a celestial angel what is celestial. Nor can they do anything other, for what they elicit is of the same type as they themselves are and is in tune with their own disposition and being.

66 But this must first be illustrated with comparisons taken from the three natural kingdoms, which are called the animal, vegetable, and mineral.

From the animal kingdom. From food reduced to chyle the vessels of the body draw and extract the blood they need, the fibres of the nerves draw their fluid, and the substances from which the fibres originate draw their animal spirit.

From the vegetable kingdom. A tree with its trunk, branches, leaves, and fruits stands upon its root, and by means of the root draws out and extracts from the soil a thick sap for the trunk, branches, and leaves, a purer sap for the flesh of the fruits, and the purest for the seeds inside the fruits.

From the mineral kingdom. There are in certain places hidden deep in the earth mineral ores rich in gold, silver, and iron; from exhalations concealed in the earth gold, silver, and iron each attract their own element.

67 Next let an example serve to show how spiritual angels draw out their sense, and celestial angels theirs, from the natural sense, the sense of the Word that people have. Let five of the Ten Commandments be the example.

Praeceptum, *Patrem tuum et matrem tuam honorabis.* Homo per patrem et matrem intelligit patrem et matrem in terra, ut et omnes qui loco patris et matris sunt, et per honorare intelligit illos honore habere et illis obedire. At angelus spiritualis per patrem intelligit Dominum et per matrem ecclesiam, et per honorare intelligit amare. Angelus autem caelestis per patrem intelligit Divinum Amorem Domini, per matrem Divinam Sapientiam Ipsius, et per honorare facere bonum ab Ipso.

Praeceptum, *Non furaberis.* Homo per furari intelligit furari, defraudare, sub aliqua specie proximo auferre sua bona. Angelus spiritualis per furari intelligit deprivare alios suae fidei veris et charitatis bonis, per falsa et mala. Angelus autem caelestis per furari intelligit attribuere sibi illa quae Domini sunt ac vindicare sibi justitiam et meritum Ipsius.

Praeceptum, *Non adulteraberis.* Homo per adulterari intelligit adulterium committere, scortari, obscaena facere, lasciva loqui, et spurca cogitare. Angelus spiritualis per adulterari intelligit adulterare bona Verbi et falsificare vera ejus. Angelus autem caelestis per adulterari intelligit negare Divinum Domini et prophanare Verbum.

Praeceptum, *Non occides.* Homo per occidere etiam intelligit odio habere, et vindictam cupere usque ad necem. Angelus spiritualis pro occidere intelligit diabolum agere et necare animam hominis. Angelus autem caelestis pro occidere intelligit Dominum odio habere et illa quae Domini sunt.

Praeceptum, *Non false testaberis.* Homo per false testari etiam intelligit mentiri et diffamare. Angelus spiritualis pro false testari intelligit dicere et persuadere quod falsum sit verum, ac malum sit bonum, et vicissim. Angelus autem caelestis pro false testari intelligit blasphemare Dominum et Verbum.

Ex his videri potest quomodo evolvitur et extrahitur spirituale et caeleste ex sensu naturali Verbi, cui insunt, et, quod mirabile est, quod angeli extrahant sua, praeter quod sciant quid homo cogitat; at usque cogitationes angelorum et hominum unum faciunt per correspondentias, sicut finis, causa, et effectus. Fines etiam actualiter sunt in regno caelesti,

1. The commandment, *You are to honour your father and your mother*. People understand by father and mother a father and mother on earth, and also everyone who stands in place of a father or mother; and by honouring they understand treating them with respect and obeying them. But spiritual angels understand by father the Lord and by mother the church; and by honouring they understand loving. Celestial angels, however, understand the Lord's Divine Love by father and His Divine Wisdom by mother, and doing the good He desires by honouring.

2. The commandment, *You are not to steal*. People by stealing understand stealing, defrauding, and depriving the neighbour of his goods on some pretext. Spiritual angels by stealing understand depriving others of the truths of their faith, and of forms of the good of charity, by false ideas and evil ways. Celestial angels, however, by stealing understand attributing to themselves what is the Lord's and claiming for themselves His righteousness and merit.

3. The commandment, *You are not to commit adultery*. People by committing adultery understand committing adultery, behaving promiscuously, doing what is obscene, making improper suggestions, and entertaining filthy thoughts. Spiritual angels by committing adultery understand adulterating forms of good upheld by the Word and falsifying its truths. Celestial angels, however, by committing adultery understand denying the Divinity of the Lord and profaning the Word.

4. The commandment, *You are not to kill*. People by killing also understand hating and wanting revenge as far as murder. Spiritual angels by killing understand playing the part of the devil and murdering a person's soul. Celestial angels, however, understand by killing hating the Lord and those things that are the Lord's.

5. The commandment, *You are not to bear false witness*. People by bearing false witness also understand telling lies and slandering. Spiritual angels by bearing false witness understand saying and persuading others that falsity is truth and evil is good, and vice versa. Celestial angels, however, by bearing false witness understand blaspheming against the Lord and the Word.

6. From these commandments it can be seen how the spiritual and celestial contents are unwound and drawn out of the natural sense of the Word, which contains them. It is a remarkable fact that the angels draw out their own senses without knowing what the person reading is thinking. Yet the thoughts of angels and people make one by means of correspondences, just as do an end, its cause, and its effect. In fact the ends are in the celestial kingdom, the causes

causae in regno spirituali, et effectus in regno naturali. Ipsa conjunctio per correspondentias talis est ex creatione. Inde nunc est consociatio cum angelis per Verbum.

68 Quod consociatio hominis cum angelis sit per sensum naturalem seu literalem Verbi, est quoque quia in unoquovis homine ex creatione sunt tres gradus vitae, caelestis, spiritualis, et naturalis; sed homo in naturali est quamdiu est in mundo, et tunc tantum in spirituali quantum in genuinis veris est et tantum in caelesti quantum in vita secundum illa est. At usque non venit in ipsum spirituale et caeleste quam post mortem. Sed de hac re plura alibi.

69 Ex his constare potest quod in solo Verbo, per id quod sit conjunctio cum Domino et consociatio cum angelis, sit spiritus et vita, sicut Dominus docet –

Verba quae Ego loquor vobis, spiritus et vita sunt. Joh.6:63.

Aqua quam Ego dabo vobis, fiet fons aquae salientis in vitam aeternam. Joh.4:14.

Homo non ex solo pane vivit sed ex omni verbo egrediente ex ore Dei. Matt.4:4.

Operamini cibum qui manet in vitam aeternam, quem Filius Hominis vobis dabit. Joh.6:27.

in the spiritual kingdom, and the effects in the natural kingdom. In itself linking by means of correspondences is such as this from creation. So it is, then, that association with angels is brought about by means of the Word.

68 The fact that people's association with angels is brought about by means of the natural or literal sense of the Word is also why in every person there are from creation three degrees of life, celestial, spiritual, and natural. But people remain in the natural degree so long as they are in the world, and at that time are in the spiritual only to the extent that they possess genuine truths and in the celestial to the extent that they lead a life guided by those truths. Yet they do not enter into the real spiritual and celestial degrees until after death. But more will be said elsewhere on this subject.

69 From all this it becomes clear that the Word alone, which produces a link with the Lord and association with angels, is the source of spirit and life, as the Lord teaches,

The words which I speak to you are spirit and life. John 6:63.
The water which I shall give you will become a spring of water rising up to give eternal life. John 4:14.
A person does not live by bread alone but by every word that comes forth out of the mouth of God. Matt.4:4.
Work for the food which lasts to eternal life, which the Son of Man will give you. John 6:27.

Quod Verbum in omnibus caelis sit et quod inde sapientia angelica

70   Quod Verbum in caelis sit, non est hactenus notum, nec potuit notum fieri quamdiu ecclesia ignoravit quod angeli et spiritus sint homines similes hominibus in mundo, et quod illis similia sint quae hominibus in omni re, cum sola differentia quod illi spirituales sint et quod omnia quae apud illos sunt ex origine spirituali sint, et quod homines in mundo naturales sint et quod omnia apud eos ex origine naturali sint. Quamdiu hoc latuit, non potuit sciri quod Verbum etiam in caelis sit et quod legatur ab angelis ibi, et quoque a spiritibus qui sub caelis sunt. Sed ne hoc lateret in perpetuum, datum est mihi in consortio esse cum angelis et spiritibus, et loqui cum illis, et videre quae apud illos, et postea referre plura quae audivi et vidi. Hoc factum est in opere **De Caelo et Inferno**, anno 1758 Londini edito, ex quo videri potest quod angeli et spiritus sint homines, et quod omnia in copia apud illos sint quae apud homines in mundo. Quod angeli et spiritus homines sint, videatur in illo opere, n.73-77 et n.453-456; quod similia sint apud illos quae apud homines in mundo, n.170-190; tum etiam quod cultus Divinus et quod praedicationes in templis apud illos sint, n.221-227; et quod scripturae et quoque libri, n.258-264; et quod Verbum, n.259.

71   Quod Verbum in caelo attinet, hoc scriptum est stylo spirituali, qui prorsus differt a stylo naturali. Stylus spiritualis consistit ex meris literis, quarum unaquaevis involvit sensum, et sunt punctationes super literis quae exaltant sensum. Literae apud angelos regni spiritualis sunt similes literis typographicis in nostro mundo, et literae apud angelos regni caelestis, quarum unaquaevis etiam involvit integrum sensum, sunt similes vetustis literis Hebraicis, inflexae vario modo, cum signis supra et intra.

19   456 *SS*, *VR*[1], *VR*[2]: 460 *VR*[3]

The Word is to be found in all the heavens and is the source of the angels' wisdom

70 It has not previously been known that the Word is to be found in the heavens, nor could it be known so long as the church was unaware that angels and spirits are human beings like those in the world and have similar surroundings in every respect like those that people have. The only difference is that they are spiritual and everything about them comes from a spiritual origin, while people in the world are natural and everything about them comes from a natural origin. So long as this fact remained hidden no one could know that the Word is also to be found in the heavens and is read by the angels there, as well as by spirits below the heavens. But to ensure that this should not remain a secret for ever, I have been allowed to enjoy the company of angels and spirits, talking with them, seeing their surroundings, and then reporting much of what I have heard and seen. I did this in the book **Heaven and Hell**, published in 1758 in London. From this book it can be seen that angels and spirits are human beings and that everything people in the world have is there in profusion for those angels and spirits. It may be seen that angels and spirits are human beings, in §§73-77 and §§453-456; that they have similar surroundings to those people have in the world, in §§170-190; also that they have Divine worship and sermons in their churches, in §§221-227; and that they have forms of writing and also books, in §§258-264, including the Word, in §259.

71 The Word in heaven is written in a spiritual style which is quite different from the natural style. The spiritual style is composed simply of letters, each of which carries a meaning, and there are points above the letters which heighten the meaning. The letters used by the angels of the spiritual kingdom resemble printed type in our world, while the letters used by the angels of the celestial kingdom, each of which too carries a full meaning, are like ancient Hebrew letters; they are variously rounded, with marks above and inside them.

Quia talis est scriptura illorum, ideo non aliqua nomina personarum et locorum in illorum Verbo sunt quae in nostro, sed pro nominibus sunt res quas significant, sicut pro Mose Verbum Historicum, pro Elia Verbum Propheticum; pro Abrahamo, Isaco, et Jacobo Dominus quoad Divinum et Divinum Humanum; pro Aharone sacerdotium, pro Davide regium, utrumque Domini; pro nominibus duodecim filiorum Jacobi, seu tribuum Israelis, varia caeli et ecclesiae; similia pro nominibus duodecim discipulorum Domini; pro Zione et Hierosolyma ecclesia quoad Verbum et quoad doctrinam e Verbo; pro terra Canaane ipsa ecclesia; pro urbibus ibi cis et trans Jordanem varia quae ecclesiae et ejus doctrinae sunt; similiter in reliquis. Simile est cum numeris; hi nec in Verbo quod in caelo est sunt, sed pro illis res quibus numeri qui in nostro Verbo sunt correspondent. Ex his constare potest quod Verbum in caelo sit Verbum correspondens nostro Verbo, et sic quod unum sint, nam correspondentiae faciunt unum.

72 Hoc mirabile est, quod Verbum in caelis ita scriptum sit ut simplices illud simpliciter intelligant ac ut sapientes sapienter, sunt enim plures punctationes et signationes super literis quae, ut dictum est, exaltant sensum. Simplices ad illas non attendunt nec illas norunt, at sapientes attendunt, quisque secundum suam sapientiam, usque ad summam. Exemplar Verbi, ab angelis a Domino inspiratis scriptum, apud unamquamque societatem caeli majorem in sacrario ejus repositum est, ne illud quoad aliquod punctum alibi immutetur. Verbum nostrum quidem in eo simile est Verbo in caelo, quod simplices illud simpliciter intelligant et sapientes sapienter; sed hoc fit alio modo.

73 Quod omnis sapientia sit angelis per Verbum, hoc fatentur ipsi, nam quantum in Verbi intellectu sunt, tantum in luce sunt. Lux caeli est Divina Sapientia, quae coram oculis eorum est lux. In sacrario in quo exemplar Verbi repositum est, est lux flammea et candida, excedens omnem gradum lucis quae extra illud in caelo est. Causa eadem est quae supra dicta, quod Dominus sit in Verbo.

Since this is the nature of writing among the angels, there are not therefore any names of persons and places in their Word as there are in ours. Instead of names there are the realities meant by these. Instead of Moses, for instance, there is the historical section of the Word; instead of Elijah, the prophetical part; instead of Abraham, Isaac, and Jacob, the Lord's Divine and Divine Human; instead of Aaron, priesthood, and instead of David, kingship, in both cases that of the Lord. Instead of the names of the twelve sons of Jacob, that is, of the tribes of Israel, there are various qualities constituting heaven and the church, and instead of the names of the Lord's twelve disciples, the same again; instead of Zion and Jerusalem, the church in respect of the Word and teaching obtained from the Word; instead of the land of Canaan, the church itself; instead of the cities in it either side of the Jordan, various aspects of the church and its teaching; and so on with all other names. It is the same with numbers. These do not exist, either, in the Word that is in heaven; instead of them there are the realities which numbers in our Word correspond to. From all this it becomes clear that the Word in heaven is a Word corresponding to our Word, and that this being so they form a single whole, for things that correspond make one.

72 It is a remarkable fact that the Word in the heavens is so written as to be understood straightforwardly by the simple and in a learned way by the wise. For it contains many points and marks over the letters which, as said before, heighten the meaning. The simple pay no attention to or know anything about them, but the wise do pay attention, each comprehending them according to their level of wisdom, even up to the highest. All the larger communities of heaven have a copy of the Word written by angels inspired by the Lord, which is kept stored in their shrine for fear that held anywhere else even a point of it should be changed. Our Word, it is true, resembles the Word in heaven insofar as the simple understand it straightforwardly and the wise in a learned way; but the way this happens is different.

73 The angels themselves declare that all their wisdom comes through the Word, for the light they enjoy depends upon how deep is their understanding of the Word. The light of heaven is Divine Wisdom, which is visible to their eyes as light. In the shrine where the copy of the Word is stored, the light is flame-like and brilliant, surpassing in intensity every degree of light in heaven outside it. The reason why is the same as that stated above, that the Lord is present in the Word.

74 Sapientia angelorum caelestium excedit sapientiam angelorum spiritualium, paene sicut sapientia angelorum spiritualium excedit sapientiam hominum, et hoc ex causa quia angeli caelestes in bono amoris a Domino sunt et angeli
5 spirituales in veris sapientiae a Domino sunt; et ubi bonum amoris est, ibi residet sapientia simul, at ubi vera sunt, ibi non residet plus sapientiae quam quantum simul bonum amoris. Haec causa est quod Verbum in regno caelesti aliter scriptum sit quam Verbum in regno spirituali, nam in Verbo regni
10 caelestis sunt expressa bona amoris, et signa sunt affectiones, at in Verbo regni spiritualis sunt expressa vera sapientiae, et signa sunt perceptiones.

75 Ex his concludi potest qualis sapientia in Verbo quod in mundo est recondita latet, in hoc enim latet omnis sapientia
15 angelica, quae ineffabilis est, est enim continens ejus, et in illam venit homo post mortem qui a Domino per Verbum angelus fit.

74 The wisdom of the celestial angels exceeds that of the spiritual angels, almost to the same extent as the wisdom of the spiritual angels exceeds people's wisdom. This is because the celestial angels have the goodness of love from the Lord and the spiritual angels have the truths of wisdom from the Lord. Where the goodness of love is, there too dwells wisdom; but where truths are, wisdom does not dwell except to the extent that the goodness of love is there too. This is why the Word is written differently in the celestial kingdom from the Word in the spiritual kingdom. For in the Word of the celestial kingdom the different kinds of the goodness of love are expressed, and the marks denote affections; but in the Word of the spiritual kingdom the truths of wisdom are expressed, and the marks denote perceptions.

75 From all this people are able to conclude what wisdom there is lying hidden within the Word that exists in the world. For in it lies hidden all the wisdom of the angels, which is beyond description; and since it contains that wisdom, those people after death enter into possession of it who by means of the Word are made angels by the Lord.

Quod ecclesia sit ex Verbo, et quod talis sit, qualis ei est intellectus Verbi

76 Quod ecclesia sit ex Verbo, hoc non venit in dubium, nam Verbum est ipsum Divinum Verum, n.1-4; ex Verbo est doctrina ecclesiae, n.50-61; et per Verbum est conjunctio cum Domino, n.62-69. Sed quod intellectus Verbi faciat ecclesiam, hoc in dubium venire potest, quoniam sunt qui credunt quod ab ecclesia sint quia Verbum habent, id legunt vel a praedicatore audiunt, et aliquid ex sensu literae ejus sciunt. Sed quomodo hoc et illud in Verbo intelligendum est, non sciunt, et quidam non tanti aestimant. Quare hic confirmabitur quod non Verbum faciat ecclesiam sed intellectus ejus, et quod ecclesia talis sit, qualis est intellectus Verbi apud illos qui in ecclesia sunt. Hoc confirmatur ex his.

77 Verbum est Verbum secundum intellectum ejus apud hominem, hoc est, sicut intelligitur. Si non intelligitur, Verbum quidem vocatur Verbum sed apud hominem non est. Verbum est veritas secundum intellectum ejus, nam potest Verbum non veritas esse, potest enim falsificari. Verbum est spiritus et vita secundum intellectum ejus, nam litera absque intellectu ejus est mortua. Quoniam homini est veritas et vita secundum intellectum Verbi, est quoque ei fides et amor secundum illum, nam veritas est fidei et amor est vitae. Nunc quia per fidem et amorem, et secundum illa, est ecclesia, sequitur quod per intellectum Verbi, et secundum illum, ecclesia sit ecclesia – ecclesia nobilis si in genuinis veris est, ignobilis si non in genuinis veris, et destructa si in falsificatis veris.

78 Praeterea Dominus apud hominem praesens est et ei conjunctus per Verbum, quoniam Dominus est Verbum et in illo quasi loquitur cum homine, tum quia Dominus est

The church owes its existence to the Word and what the church is like depends on its understanding of the Word

76   There can be no doubt that the church owes its existence to the Word, for the Word is Divine Truth itself, §§1-4; the Word is the source of the church's teaching, §§50-61; and the Word produces a link with the Lord, §§62-69. However, it may be questioned whether it is the understanding of the Word which makes the church, since there are those who believe that they belong to the church because they possess the Word, read it or hear it preached, and know something of its literal sense. But they are unaware how this or that passage in the Word is to be understood, and some of them do not regard this to be of much importance. Here therefore it will be shown clearly that it is not the Word which makes the church but the understanding of it does so, and that what the church is like depends on the understanding of the Word by those who belong to the church. The following considerations clearly show this to be so.

77   The Word is the Word according to people's understanding of it, that is, the way they understand it. If they have no understanding of it, the Word is indeed called the Word, but it does not dwell with them. The Word is truth according to the understanding of it, for it is possible for the Word not to be truth, since it can be falsified. The Word is spirit and life according to the understanding of it, for without any understanding of the Word the literal sense is dead. Since people have truth and life according to their understanding of the Word they also have faith and love according to it, because truth and faith go together, as do love and life. Now because it is through and according to faith and love that the church is in existence it follows that it is through and according to its understanding of the Word that a church is the kind of church it is – an excellent church if it possesses genuine truths, a worthless one if it possesses truths that are not genuine, and a ruined one if it possesses falsified truths.

78   Furthermore the Lord is present with and linked to people through the Word because the Lord is the Word and within it He, as it were, talks to them, and for the reason as well that the Lord is

ipsum Divinum Verum, et quoque Verbum est illud. Ex hoc patet quod Dominus apud hominem praesens sit, et simul illi conjunctus, secundum intellectum Verbi, nam secundum illum est homini veritas et inde fides, tum etiam amor et inde vita. Sed est Dominus praesens apud hominem per lectionem Verbi, at ei conjunctus per intellectum veri ex Verbo et secundum illum; et quantum Dominus homini conjunctus est, tantum in homine est ecclesia. Ecclesia est in homine; ecclesia quae extra illum est, est ecclesia apud plures in quibus est ecclesia. Hoc intelligitur per Domini verba ad Pharisaeos interrogantes quando venit regnum Dei,

Regnum Dei intra vos est. Luc.17:21.

Per regnum Dei intelligitur ibi Dominus, et ab Ipso ecclesia.

79   In multis locis apud Prophetas agitur de intellectu Verbi ubi agitur de ecclesia, et docetur quod non alibi sit ecclesia quam ubi Verbum juste intelligitur, et quod talis sit ecclesia, qualis est intellectus Verbi apud illos qui in illa sunt. Multis in locis apud Prophetas etiam describitur ecclesia apud gentem Israeliticam et Judaicam, quod prorsus destructa et nulla facta sit per id quod sensum seu intellectum Verbi falsificaverint, nam aliud non destruit ecclesiam.

Intellectus Verbi, tam verus quam falsus, describitur apud Prophetas per Ephraimum, imprimis apud Hoscheam, nam per Ephraimum in Verbo significatur intellectus Verbi in ecclesia. Et quia intellectus Verbi facit ecclesiam, ideo Ephraim vocatur, Filius pretiosus, et Natus delitiarum, Jer.31:20; Primogenitus, Jer.31:9; Robur capitis Jehovae, Ps.60:9; Ps.108:9; Potens, Sach.10:7; Impletus arcu, Sach.9:13. Et filii Ephraimi vocantur, Armati et Jaculatores arcus, Ps.78:9. Per arcum significatur doctrina ex Verbo pugnans contra falsa. Ideo etiam Ephraim ad dextram Israelis translatus est, et benedictus; tum loco Rubenis acceptatus, Gen.48:5,11,seq. Et ideo Ephraim una cum fratre suo Menasse, a Mose in benedictione filiorum Israelis sub nomine Josephi patris illorum supra omnes exaltatus est, Deut.33:13-17.

Divine Truth itself, which also constitutes the Word. From this it is evident that the Lord is present with and at the same time linked to people according to their understanding of the Word, since it is according to this that people are in possession of truth and therefore faith, and also love and therefore life. However, the Lord is present with people through the reading of the Word, but linked to them through and according to their understanding of truth obtained from the Word. And to the extent that the Lord is linked to people, to the same extent they have the church within them. The church exists within people; and the church outside them is the church with the very many who have the church within them. This is the meaning of the Lord's words to the Pharisees who asked when does God's kingdom come,

The kingdom of God is within you. Luke 17:21.

Here the kingdom of God means the Lord and the church that exists from Him.

79 Many places in the Prophets in which the church is the subject relate to the understanding of the Word. The teaching in them is that the church exists only where the Word is rightly understood and that the character of a church depends on what kind of understanding of the Word exists among those in that church. Many places too in the Prophets describe how the church among the Israelite and Jewish nation was utterly destroyed and annihilated by their falsifying the meaning or understanding of the Word, for nothing other than this destroys a church.

2   The understanding of the Word, both true and false, is described in the Prophets, especially Hosea, by Ephraim, for Ephraim stands in the Word for the understanding of the Word in the church. And because the understanding of the Word makes the church Ephraim is called a precious son and a delightful child, Jer.31:20; the firstborn, Jer.31:9; the strength of Jehovah's head, Ps.60:7; Ps.108:8; a powerful one, Zech.10:7; one armed with the bow, Zech.9:13. Also, the sons of Ephraim are called armed men and shooters of the bow, Ps.78:9. A bow means teaching from the Word militating against falsities. For the same reason too Ephraim was transferred to Israel's right hand and blessed, and also received in place of Reuben, Gen.48:5,11, and following verses. And again for the same reason Ephraim together with his brother Manasseh was raised above all others by Moses when he blessed the sons of Israel in the name of Joseph their father, Deut.33:13-17.

Qualis autem ecclesia est quando intellectus Verbi est deperditus, per Ephraimum etiam apud Prophetas describitur, imprimis apud Hoscheam, ut patet ex his –

Israel et Ephraim corruent. Ephraim in solitudinem erit. Ephraim oppressus et concussus judicii. Ego ero ut leo Ephraimo, rapiam et ibo, auferam et non eripiens. Hos.5:5,9,11-14.
Quid faciam tibi Ephraim? Quia sanctitas tua, sicut nubes aurorae et sicut ros mane cadens, abit. Hos.6:4.
Non habitabunt in terra Jehovae; revertetur Ephraim in Aegyptum, et in Assyria immundum comedet. Hos.9:3.

Terra Jehovae est ecclesia, Aegyptus est scientificum naturalis hominis, Assyria est ratiocinatio inde, ex quibus Verbum quoad intellectum ejus falsificatur. Ideo dicitur quod Ephraim in Aegyptum revertetur, et in Assyria immundum comedet.

Ephraim pascens ventum, et persequitur eurum; omni die mendacium et vastationem multiplicat; faedus cum Assyrio pangit, et oleum in Aegyptum defertur. Hos.12:2.

Pascere ventum, persequi eurum, ac multiplicare mendacium et vastationem, est falsificare vera, et sic destruere ecclesiam.
Simile etiam significatur per scortationem Ephraimi – nam scortatio significat falsificationem intellectus Verbi, hoc est, genuini veri ejus – in his,

Ego novi Ephraimum, quod omnino scortatus sit, et pollutus sit Israel. Hos.5:3.
In domo Israelis vidi rem faedam; ibi scortatus est Ephraim, et pollutus est Israel. Hos.6:10.

Israel est ipsa ecclesia, et Ephraim est intellectus Verbi, ex quo et secundum quem est ecclesia, quare dicitur, Scortatus est Ephraim, et pollutus est Israel.
Quoniam ecclesia apud Judaeos per falsificationes Verbi plane destructa fuit, ideo de Ephraimo ita dicitur,

Dabo te Ephraim, tradam te Israel, sicut Adamam; et ponam te sicut Zeboim. Hos.11:8.

9 Ephraim in Aegyptum SS^3: Ephraim Aegyptum SS^1, SS^2

What the church, however, is like when its understanding of 3
the Word is destroyed is also described in the Prophets by Ephraim,
especially in Hosea, as is evident in the following places,

Israel and Ephraim will collapse. Ephraim will be a wilderness. Ephraim
is oppressed and shaken in judgment. I will be like a lion to Ephraim, I
will tear and go away, I will carry off with no one coming to the rescue.
Hos.5:5,9,11-14.
What shall I do to you, Ephraim? For your holiness goes away, like the
clouds of dawn and like the dew that falls in the morning. Hos.6:4.
They will not dwell in the land of Jehovah; Ephraim will return to Egypt,
and in Assyria will eat what is unclean. Hos.9:3.

The land of Jehovah is the church, Egypt is factual knowledge 4
present on the natural level of the human mind, Assyria is reasoning
based on it, which knowledge and reasoning lead to falsification of
the Word in respect of the understanding of it. This is why it says that
Ephraim will return to Egypt, and in Assyria will eat what is unclean.

Ephraim pastures the wind and pursues the east wind; every day he 5
increases the lie and devastation; he makes a covenant with Assyria and
oil is carried into Egypt. Hos.12:1.

Pasturing the wind, pursuing the east wind, and increasing the lie
and devastation is falsifying truths and so destroying the church.

Ephraim's whoring has a similar meaning, for whoring 6
means the falsification of the understanding of the Word, that is, of
its genuine truth, in the following places –

I know Ephraim, that he has utterly given himself to whoring, and Israel
is defiled. Hos.5:3
In the house of Israel I have seen a foul thing; there Ephraim went
whoring and Israel is defiled. Hos.6:10.

Israel is the church itself, and Ephraim is the understanding of the
Word, the source which determines what sort of church it is. This is
why it says that Ephraim went whoring and Israel is defiled.

Because the church was utterly destroyed among the Jews 7
by falsifications of the Word the following is said of Ephraim,

I shall give you up, Ephraim, I shall hand you over, Israel, like Admah;
and I shall make you like Zeboiim. Hos.11:8.

Nunc quia apud Prophetam Hoscheam, a primo capite ad ultimum ibi, agitur de falsificatione Verbi et de destructione ecclesiae per illam, et quia per scortationem significatur falsificatio veri ibi, ideo mandatum est illi prophetae ut
5 representaret illum statum ecclesiae per quod acciperet sibi scortum in mulierem, et ex illa gigneret filios, cap.1, ac iterum, ut acciperet mulierem adulteram, cap.3.

Haec allata sunt ut ex Verbo sciatur et confirmetur quod ecclesia talis sit, qualis est intellectus Verbi in illa, praestans
10 et pretiosa si intellectus ejus sit ex genuinis veris ex Verbo, at destructa, imo foeda, si ex falsificatis. Ad confirmationem quod per Ephraimum significetur intellectus Verbi, et in opposito sensu ille falsificatus, et quod inde sit destructio ecclesiae, conferri possunt reliqua loca in quibus de Ephraimo
15 agitur, ut,

Hos.4:17,18; 7:1,11; 8:9,11; 9:11-13,16; 10:11; 11:3; 12:1,9,15; 13:1,12; Esai.17:3; 28:1; Jer.4:15; 31:6,18; 50:19; Ezech.37:16; 48:5; Obad. vers.19; Sach.9:10.

Now because the subject in the book of the prophet Hosea from the first chapter to the last is the falsification of the Word and the resulting destruction of the church, and because whoring there means the falsification of truth, that is why this prophet was commanded to represent that state of the church by marrying a woman who was a whore and having children by her, in chapter 1, and again to marry an adulterous woman, in chapter 3.

These places have been quoted to provide knowledge and evidence from the Word that what the church is like depends on how the Word is understood in it. It is excellent and valuable if its understanding is based on genuine truths from the Word, but ruined and actually foul if based on falsified ones. All the other places in which Ephraim is referred to may be assembled as evidence that the understanding of the Word is meant by Ephraim, or in a contrary sense a falsified understanding of it, which leads to the destruction of the church, for instance –

Hos.4:17,18; 7:1,11; 8:9,11; 9:11-13,16; 10:11; 11:3,12; 12:8,14; 13:1,12; Isa.17:3; 28:1; Jer.4:15; 31:6,18; 50:19; Ezek.37:16; 48:5; Obad. verse 19; Zech.9:10.

Quod in singulis Verbi sit conjugium Domini et ecclesiae et inde conjugium boni et veri

80   Quod in singulis Verbi sit conjugium Domini et ecclesiae et inde conjugium boni et veri, hactenus non visum est; nec videri potuit, quia sensus spiritualis Verbi non prius detectus est, et id non videri potest nisi per illum. Sunt enim bini sensus in Verbo latentes in sensu literae ejus, spiritualis et caelestis. In spirituali sensu se referunt illa quae in Verbo sunt, maxime ad ecclesiam, et in caelesti, maxime ad Dominum; tum in spirituali sensu se referunt illa ad Divinum Verum et in caelesti ad Divinum Bonum. Inde est in sensu literae Verbi illud conjugium. Sed hoc non apparet alicui nisi qui ex sensu spirituali et caelesti Verbi scit vocum et nominum significationes, nam quaedam voces et nomina praedicantur de bono et quaedam de vero, et quaedam includunt utrumque, quare absque illa cognitione conjugium illud in singulis Verbi non videri potuit. Haec causa est quod hoc arcanum non prius detectum fuerit.

81   Quia tale conjugium in singulis Verbi est, ideo multoties in Verbo sunt binae expressiones quae apparent sicut repetitiones ejusdem rei, attamen non sunt repetitiones sed una se refert ad bonum et altera ad verum, et utraque simul sumta facit conjunctionem illorum, ita unam rem. Inde etiam est Divinitas Verbi, et Sanctitas ejus, nam in omni opere Divino est bonum conjunctum vero et verum conjunctum bono.

82   Dicitur quod in singulis Verbi sit conjugium Domini et ecclesiae, et inde conjugium boni et veri, quia ubi conjugium Domini et ecclesiae est, ibi etiam conjugium boni et veri est, est enim hoc ab illo. Nam cum ecclesia seu homo ecclesiae in veris est, tunc Dominus in vera ejus influit cum bono et illa vivificat, seu, quod idem, cum ecclesia seu homo ecclesiae per vera in intelligentia est, tunc Dominus per

The details of the Word all contain a marriage of the Lord and the church and so a marriage of goodness and truth

80   Up to now it has not been seen that the details of the Word contain a marriage of the Lord and the church, and so a marriage of goodness and truth. Nor could this be seen, because the spiritual sense of the Word has not before been revealed, and the marriage can be seen only by means of that sense. For the Word has two senses hidden in its literal sense, the spiritual and the celestial. In the spiritual sense the contents of the Word refer chiefly to the church, and in the celestial chiefly to the Lord. Again in the spiritual sense its contents refer to Divine Truth and the celestial to Divine Goodness. So that marriage is present within the literal sense of the Word. But this is not apparent except to those who have learned from the spiritual and celestial senses of the Word the meanings of the words and names. For certain words and names are used of goodness, and certain of truth, and some include both. So without this knowledge it was impossible to see this marriage in the details of the Word. This is the reason why the secret was not previously revealed.

81   It is because this kind of marriage is contained in the details of the Word that it so often uses two expressions which appear to repeat the same thing. Yet they are not really repetitions but one refers to goodness and the other to truth, and the two taken together make this link and so form a single unit. This too is the reason why the Word is Divine and holy, for in every Divine act goodness is wedded to truth and truth to goodness.

82   There is said to be a marriage of the Lord and the church in the details of the Word, and consequently a marriage of goodness and truth, because where there is a marriage of the Lord and the church, there too is a marriage of goodness and truth, for the latter is the result of the former. When a church, that is, its members, are in possession of truths, the Lord acts upon its truths with goodness and makes them come alive, or, what is the same thing, when a church or its members are in possession of understanding gained

bonum amoris et charitatis in intelligentiam ejus influit et sic ei infundit vitam.

83 Sunt binae facultates vitae apud unumquemvis hominem, quae vocantur intellectus et voluntas. Intellectus est receptaculum veri et inde sapientiae, et voluntas est receptaculum boni et inde amoris. Haec unum facient, ut homo sit homo ecclesiae, ac unum faciunt dum homo intellectum format ex genuinis veris, et hoc fit ad apparentiam sicut ab illo, et dum voluntas ejus impletur bono amoris, hoc fit a Domino. Inde homini vita veri et vita boni est, vita veri in intellectu ex voluntate et vita boni in voluntate per intellectum. Hoc est conjugium veri et boni apud hominem, tum conjugium Domini et ecclesiae apud illum. Sed de reciproca hac conjunctione, quae hic vocatur conjugium, in Sapientia Angelica de **Divina Providentia**, de **Divino Amore et de Divina Sapientia**, et de **Vita** videbitur.

84 Quod in Verbo sint binae expressiones quae apparent sicut repetitiones ejusdem rei, a legentibus qui ad id attendunt, potest videri; ut frater et socius, pauper et egenus, vastitas et solitudo, vacuitas et inanitas, hostis et inimicus, peccatum et iniquitas, ira et excandescentia, gens et populus, gaudium et laetitia, luctus et lachrymatio, justitia et judicium, etc., quae apparent sicut synonyma, cum tamen usque non sunt. Nam frater, pauper, vastitas, vacuitas, hostis, peccatum, ira, gens, gaudium, luctus, justitia praedicantur de bono et in opposito sensu de malo, at socius, egenus, solitudo, inanitas, inimicus, iniquitas, excandescentia, populus, laetitia, lachrymatio, judicium praedicantur de vero et in opposito sensu de falso. Et tamen apparet legenti qui hoc arcanum non novit, quod pauper et egenus, vastitas et solitudo, vacuitas et inanitas, hostis et inimicus, una res sint, similiter peccatum et iniquitas, ira et excandescentia, gens et populus, gaudium et laetitia, luctus et lachrymatio, justitia et judicium; et tamen non una res sunt, sed una res fiunt per conjunctionem.

In Verbo etiam conjunguntur plura, ut ignis et flamma, aurum et argentum, aes et ferrum, lignum et lapis, panis et

---

19 et socius, pauper SS^3, VR: om SS^1, SS^2
24 vacuitas SS^3, VR^3: om SS^1, SS^2, VR^1, VR^2

through truths, the Lord acts on their understanding by means of the goodness of love and charity and thus pours life into it.

83 Every person has two faculties of life, known as the understanding and the will. The understanding receives truth and consequently wisdom, the will receives goodness and consequently love. These must act as one for a person to be a true member of the church, and they do act as one so long as people form their understanding from genuine truths, and this appears to be their own doing, and so long as their will is filled with the goodness of love, which is the Lord's doing. People therefore have a life of truth and a life of goodness – the life of truth in the understanding rooted in the will, and the life of goodness in the will coming through the understanding. This is the marriage of truth and goodness in someone, and also the marriage of the Lord and the church in the person. But more about this reciprocal bond, which is being called a marriage here, will appear in Angelic Wisdom concerning **Divine Providence**, concerning **Divine Love and Wisdom**, and concerning **Life**.[1]

84 Attentive readers may observe that there seem to be pairs of expressions in the Word which look like repetitions of the same thing. For instance, brother and companion, poor and needy, wilderness and uninhabited place, void and emptiness, enemy and opponent, sin and iniquity, anger and wrath, nation and people, joy and gladness, grief and weeping, righteousness and judgment, etc. These appear to be synonyms, yet they are not. For brother, poor, wilderness, void, enemy, sin, anger, nation, joy, grief, and righteousness are used in speaking of goodness, and in the opposite sense of badness. But companion, needy, uninhabited place, emptiness, opponent, iniquity, wrath, people, gladness, weeping, and judgment are used in speaking of truth, and in the opposite sense of falsity. Yet it looks to the reader who does not know this secret that poor and needy, wilderness and uninhabited place, void and emptiness, enemy and opponent are one and the same thing; similarly so, sin and iniquity, anger and wrath, nation and people, joy and gladness, grief and weeping, righteousness and judgment. However they are not one and the same thing, but are linked together to make a single thing.

Many more expressions in the Word are coupled, like fire and flame, gold and silver, bronze and iron, wood and stone, bread

---

[1] Here Swedenborg was referring to the sixth, eighth, and ninth of the subjects which – he stated in his Preface to **Doctrina Novae Hierosolymae de Domino** (**DD**) – he was intending to deal with in forthcoming works

aqua, panis et vinum, purpura et byssus, etc., et hoc, quia ignis, aurum, aes, lignum, panis, purpura significant bonum, ac flamma, argentum, ferrum, lapis, aqua, vinum, et byssus significant verum. Similiter, quod dicatur quod amaturi sint Deum ex toto corde et ex tota anima, tum quod Deus creaturus sit in homine novum cor et novum spiritum, cor enim praedicatur de bono amoris, anima de vero ex illo bono. Sunt etiam voces quae quia de utroque tam bono quam vero participant, solitarie absque adjunctis aliis dicuntur. Sed haec et plura alia non exstant nisi coram angelis, et coram illis qui, dum in sensu naturali, etiam in sensu spirituali sunt.

85   Quod binae tales expressiones in Verbo sint quae apparent sicut repetitiones ejusdem rei, prolixum foret ex Verbo ostendere, nam chartas impleret. Sed ut tollatur dubium, velim loca afferre ubi **Judicium** et **Justitia** simul dicuntur, tum ubi **Gens** et **Populus**, ut et ubi **Gaudium** et **Laetitia**.

Loca ubi **Judicium** et simul **Justitia** nominantur, haec sint–

Urbs plena erat **judicio**, **justitia** pernoctabat. Esai.1:21.
Zion in **judicio** redimetur, et reduces ejus in **justitia**. Esai.1:27.
Exaltetur Jehovah Zebaoth in **judicio**, et Deus sanctus sanctificetur in **justitia**. Esai.5:16.
Sedebit super throno Davidis et super regno ejus, ad stabiliendum illud in **judicio** et in **justitia**. Esai.9:6.
Exaltetur Jehovah, quia inhabitat altum et implevit Zionem **judicio** et **justitia**. Esai.33:5.
Dixit Jehovah, Custodite **judicium** et facite **justitiam**, quia prope est **salus** Mea ut **justitia** Mea Reveletur. Esai.56:1.
Quasi gens quae **justitiam** facit, et **judicium** Dei sui non deseruit, rogent **judicia justitiae**. Esai.58:2.
Jura per vivum Jehovam, in **judicio** et in **justitia**. Jer.4:2.
De hoc glorietur qui gloriatur, quod Jehovah faciat **judicium** et **justitiam** in terra. Jer.9:23.
Facite **judicium** et **justitiam**. Vae aedificanti domum suam sine **justitia**, et hyperoa sua sine **judicio**. Nonne pater tuus fecit **judicium** et **justitiam**, et tunc bene illi? Jer.22:3,13,15.

19   judicio: justitia *SS*
19   justitia: judicio *SS*
24   Zionem: terram *SS*
28   facit: fecit *SS*
33   Facite *SS*³: Facito *SS*¹, *SS*²

and water, bread and wine, purple and fine linen, etc. The reason for this is that fire, gold, bronze, wood, bread, and purple stand for goodness, while flame, silver, iron, stone, water, wine, and fine linen stand for truth. Similarly when it says that people are to love God with all their heart and with all their soul, or that God will create in a person a new heart and a new spirit. The heart is used in speaking of the goodness of love, the soul of the truth rooted in that goodness. There are also expressions which are used by themselves without other additions, because they relate to both goodness and truth; but these and many other things do not become evident except to angels, and to those who, while having the natural sense, are also able to receive the spiritual sense.

85 To demonstrate from the Word that it contains pairs of expressions which look like repetitions of the same thing would be tedious, since it would fill pages. But in order to remove any doubt I would like to quote places where **Judgment** and **Righteousness** are mentioned together, also **Nation** and **People**, and as well **Joy** and **Gladness**.

Places in which **Judgment** and **Righteousness** are named together are the following –

The city was full of **judgment**, **righteousness** spent the night. Isa.1:21.
Zion will be redeemed with **judgment**, and returners with **righteousness**. Isa.1:27.
Let Jehovah Zebaoth be exalted in **judgment**, and let the holy God be hallowed in **righteousness**. Isa.5:16.
He will sit upon the throne of David and over his kingdom, to establish it with **judgment** and with **righteousness**. Isa.9:7.
Let Jehovah be exalted, for He dwells on high and has filled Zion with **judgment** and **righteousness**. Isa.33:5.
Jehovah said, Keep **judgment** and execute **righteousness**, for My **salvation** is near so that My **righteousness** may be revealed. Isa.56:1.
As a nation that does **righteousness**, and has not forsaken the **judgment** of its God, let them ask of the **judgments of righteousness**. Isa.58:2.
Swear by the living Jehovah, in **judgment** and in **righteousness**. Jer.4:2.
Let those who boast boast in this, that Jehovah executes **judgment** and **righteousness** in the earth. Jer.9:24.
Execute **judgment** and **righteousness**. Woe to those who build their house without **righteousness**, and their upper rooms without **judgment**. Did not your father execute **judgment** and **righteousness**, and then it was well for him? Jer.22:3,13,15.

DOCTRINA DE SCRIPTURA SACRA

Suscitabo Davidi germen justum qui regnet Rex, et faciet **judicium** et **justitiam** in terra. Jer.23:5; 33:15.
Si vir fuerit justus, qui fecerit **judicium** et **justitiam**, ... Ezech.18:5.
Si impius reversus fuerit, et fecerit **judicium** et **justitiam**, non fiet
5 mentio contra eum; **judicium** et **justitiam** fecit, vivendo vivet. Ezech.33:14,16,19.
Desponsabo te Mihi in aeternum in **justitia** et in **judicio**; et in **misericordia** et in **miserationibus**. Hos.2:19.
Fluat sicut aqua **judicium**, et **justitia** sicut torrens fortis. Amos 5:24.
10 Convertistis **judicium** in fel, et fructum **justitiae** in absinthium. Amos 6:12.
Jehovah litiget litem meam, et faciat **judicium** mihi, et educat me in lucem, et videam **justitiam** Ipsius. Mic.7:9.
Jehovah, **justitia** Tua sicut montes Dei, **judicia** Tua abyssus magna.
15 Ps.36:7.
Jehovah educet sicut lucem **justitiam** tuam, et **judicium** tuum sicut meridiem. Ps.37:6.
Jehovah judicabit populum tuum in **justitia**, et miseros tuos in **judicio**. Ps72:2.
20 **Justitia** et **judicium** fulcrum throni tui. Ps.89:15.
Cum didicero **judicia justitiae** Tuae ... Septies in die laudo Te, super **judiciis justitiae** Tuae. Ps.119:7,164.
Gad **justitiam** Jehovae fecit, et **judicia** Ipsius cum Israele. Deut.33:21.
Spiritus veritatis arguet mundum de **justitia** et de **judicio**. Joh.16:8,10.
25 Et alibi.

Quod judicium et justitia toties dicantur, est quia judicium dicitur de veris et justitia de bono, quare per facere judicium et justitiam etiam intelligitur facere ex vero et ex bono. Quod judicium dicatur de vero et justitia de bono, est
30 quia regimen Domini in regno spirituali vocatur **judicium**, et regimen Domini in regno caelesti vocatur **justitia**, de quo videatur in opere **De Caelo et Inferno**, n.214,215. Quia judicium dicitur de vero, ideo in quibusdam locis dicitur **veritas** et **justitia**, ut Esai.11:5; Ps.85:12; et alibi.

1	faciet: faciat *SS*	
7	te Mihi: Me tibi *SS*	
9	Fluat: Fluet *SS*	
16	tuam *SS*³: suam *SS*¹, *SS*²	
16	tuum *SS*³: om *SS*¹, *SS*²	
18	tuum: suum *SS*	
18	tuos: suos *SS*	
23	fecit: facit *SS*	

TEACHING CONCERNING SACRED SCRIPTURE	n.85

I will raise up for David a righteous branch, who will reign as King and execute **judgment** and **righteousness** in the land. Jer.23:5; 33:15.
If a man has been righteous, one who has executed **judgment** and **righteousness**, ... Ezek.18:5.
If wicked people turn away from their sin and execute **judgment** and **righteousness**, it will not be remembered against them; they have executed **judgment** and **righteousness**, they will surely live. Ezek.33:14,16,19.
I will betroth you to Me for ever in **righteousness** and in **judgment**, and in **mercy** and in **compassion**. Hos.2:19.
Let **judgment** flow like water, and **righteousness** like a mighty torrent. Amos 5:24.
You have turned **judgment** into poison and the fruit of **righteousness** into wormwood. Amos 6:12.
[Until] Jehovah pleads my cause, and executes **judgment** for me, and brings me out to the light, and I see His **righteousness**. Mic.7:9.
O Jehovah, Your **righteousness** is like the mountains of God, Your **judgments** like the great abyss. Ps.36:6.
Jehovah will bring forth your **righteousness** as the light, and your **judgment** as the noonday. Ps.37:6.
Jehovah will judge your people in **righteousness**, and your needy ones in **judgment**. Ps.72:2.
Righteousness and **judgment** are the support of Your throne. Ps.89:14.
When I shall have learned Your **righteous judgments** ... Seven times a day I praise You because of Your **righteous judgments**. Ps.119:7,164.
Gad executed the **righteousness** of Jehovah, and His **judgments** with Israel. Deut.33:21.
The Spirit of truth will convict the world concerning **righteousness** and **judgment**. John 16:8,10.
And other places.

Judgment and righteousness are mentioned so many times because judgment has reference to truths and righteousness to goodness, and therefore also executing judgment and righteousness means doing so from the standpoint of truth and goodness. Judgment has reference to truth and righteousness to goodness for the reason that the Lord's government in the spiritual kingdom is termed **judgment**, and the Lord's government in the celestial kingdom is termed **righteousness**, for which, see the work **Heaven and Hell**, §§214-215. Since judgment has reference to truth, the expressions **truth** and **righteousness** are therefore used in certain places, for instance, Isa.11:5; Ps.85:11; and elsewhere.

86   Quod repetitiones sicut ejusdem rei, propter conjugium boni et veri, in Verbo sint, clarius potest videri ex locis ubi dicuntur **Gentes** et **Populi**, ut in his –

Vae **genti** peccatrici, **populo** gravi iniquitate. Esai.1:4.
Populi ambulantes in tenebris viderunt lucem magnam; multiplicasti **gentem**. Esai.9:1,2.
Aschur virga irae Meae. Contra **gentem** hypocriticam mittam illum, contra **populum** excandescentiae Meae mandabo illum. Esai.10:5,6.
Fiet in die illo, radicem Jischaji, quae stans in signum **populorum**, **gentes** quaerent. Esai.11:10.
Jehovah percutiens **populos** plaga non curabili, dominans cum ira **gentibus**. Esai.14:6.
In die illo adducetur munus Jehovae Zebaoth, **populus** distractus et expilatus, et **gens** delineata et conculcata. Esai.18:7.
Honorabunt Te **populus** validus, urbs **gentium** potentium timebunt Te. Esai.25:3.
Jehovah absorbebit obvolutionem super omnes **populos**, et velamen super omnes **gentes**. Esai.25:7.
Appropinquate, **gentes**; et **populi**, auscultate. Esai.34:1.
Vocavi Te in foedus **populo**, in lucem **gentium**. Esai.42:6.
Omnes **gentes** congregentur una, et conveniant **populi**. Esai.43:9.
Ecce tollam erga **gentes** manum Meam, et erga **populos** signum Meum. Esai.49:22.
En testem **populis** dedi Ipsum, principem et legislatorem **gentibus**. Esai.55:4,5.
Ecce **populus** veniens e terra septentrionis et **gens** magna e lateribus terrae. Jer.6:22,23.
Non audire te faciam amplius calumniam **gentium**, et opprobrium **populorum** non portabis amplius. Ezech.36:15.
Omnes **populi** et **gentes** Ipsum colent. Dan.7:14.
Ne dicterium de illis faciant **gentes**, et dixerint in **populis**, Ubi Deus eorum? Joel 2:17.
Reliquiae **populi** Mei depraedabuntur illos, et residui **gentis** Meae haereditabunt eos. Zeph.2:9.
Venient **populi** multi et **gentes** numerosae ad quaerendum Jehovam Zebaoth in Hierosolyma. Sach.8:22.

9   quae: qui SS
24   En: In SS

86. The fact that the marriage of goodness and truth is the reason for the existence in the Word of apparent repetitions of the same thing can be seen quite clearly in places where the expressions **Nations** and **Peoples** are used, for instance in the following –

Woe to a sinful **nation**, a **people** laden with iniquity. Isa.1:4.
The **peoples** walking in darkness have seen a great light; You have multiplied the **nation**. Isa.9:2,3.
O Assyria, the rod of My anger. Against a hypocritical **nation** will I send him, against the **people** of My wrath will I command him. Isa.10:5,6.
It will happen on that day, that the **nations** will seek the root of Jesse which is standing as an ensign of the **peoples**. Isa.11:10.
Jehovah is striking the **peoples** with an incurable stroke, ruling with anger the **nations**. Isa.14:6.
On that day there will be brought as a gift to Jehovah Zebaoth a **people** torn apart and pillaged, and a **nation** measured out and trampled. Isa.18:7.
A strong **people** will honour You, the city of powerful **nations** will fear You. Isa.25:3.
Jehovah will swallow up the veil over all **peoples**, and the pall over all **nations**. Isa.25:7.
Draw near, O **nations**, and listen, O **peoples**. Isa.34:1.
I have called You to be a covenant to the **people**, a light of the **nations**. Isa.42:6.
Let all the **nations** be gathered together, and let the **peoples** assemble. Isa.43:9.
Behold, I will raise My hand towards the **nations**, and My ensign towards the **peoples**. Isa.49:22.
Lo, I have given Him as a witness to the **peoples**, a prince and lawgiver to the **nations**. Isa.55:4,5.
Behold, a **people** coming from the land of the north and a mighty **nation** from the furthest parts of the earth. Jer.6:22,23.
I will cause you not to hear any longer the slander of the **nations**, and you will no longer bear the reproach of the **peoples**. Ezek.36:15.
All **peoples** and **nations** will worship Him. Dan.7:14.
Lest the **nations** make a byword of them, and say among the **peoples**, Where is their God? Joel 2:17.
The remnant of My **people** will plunder them, and the residue of My **nation** will possess them. Zeph.2:9.
Many **peoples** and numerous **nations** will come to seek Jehovah Zebaoth in Jerusalem. Zech.8:22.

Viderunt oculi mei salutare Tuum quod praeparasti ante faciem omnium **populorum**, lumen in revelationem **gentium**. Luc.2:30-32.
Redemisti nos sanguine Tuo ex omni **populo** et **gente**. Apoc.5:9.
Oportet te rursus prophetare super **populos** et **gentes**. Apoc.10:11.
Pones me in caput **gentium**; **populus** quem non noveram servient Mihi. Ps.18:44.
Jehovah irritum reddit consilium **gentium**, subvertit cogitationes **populorum**. Ps.33:10.
Ponis nos proverbium inter **gentes**, motionem capitis inter **populos**. Ps.44:15.
Jehovah subjiciet **populos** sub nos et **gentes** sub pedes nostros. Regnavit Deus super **gentes**. Spontanei **populorum** congregati sunt. Ps.47:4,9,10.
Confitebuntur Te **populi**, laetabuntur et jubilabunt **gentes**; eo quod judicaturus sis **populos** rectitudine, et **gentes** in terra ducturus sis. Ps.67:3-5.
Memento mei, Jehovah, in beneplacito **populi** Tui, ut laeter in gaudio **gentium** Tuarum. Ps.106:4,5.
Praeter alibi.

Quod gentes et simul populi dicantur, est quia per gentes intelliguntur qui in bono sunt et in opposito sensu qui in malo, et per populos qui in veris et in opposito sensu qui in falsis. Quare illi qui e spirituali regno Domini sunt vocantur populi, et illi qui e caelesti regno Domini sunt vocantur gentes, nam in spirituali regno sunt omnes in veris et inde in sapientia, in caelesti autem regno sunt omnes in bono et inde in amore.

87 Simile est cum reliquis, sicut quod ubi dicitur **Gaudium** etiam dicatur **Laetitia**, ut in his –

Ecce **gaudium** et **laetitia**; occidere bovem. Esai.22:13.
Gaudium et **laetitia** assequentur, fugient tristitia et gemitus. Esai.35:10; 51:11.
Excisum est e domo Dei nostri **laetitia** et **gaudium**. Joel 1:16.
Abrogabitur vox **gaudii** et vox **laetitiae**. Jer.7:34; 25:10.
Jejunium decimi erit domui Jehudae in **gaudium** et **laetitiam**. Sach.8:19.

---

12 Deus: Jehovah *SS, VR*
15 ducturus sis *VR*: ducturus es *SS*

My eyes have seen Your salvation, which You have prepared before the face of all **peoples**, a light to be a revelation to the **nations**. Luke 2:30-32.
You have redeemed us by Your blood from every **people** and **nation**. Rev.5:9.
You must prophesy again over the **peoples** and **nations**. Rev.10:11.
You will set me to be the head of the **nations**; a **people** whom I have not known will serve me. Ps.18:43.
Jehovah makes vain the counsel of the **nations**, overthrows the thoughts of the **peoples**. Ps.33:10.
You make us a proverb among the **nations**, a shaking of the head among the **peoples**. Ps.44:14.
Jehovah will subdue the **peoples** under us, and the **nations** under our feet. God has become king over the **nations**. The willing ones of the **peoples** have assembled. Ps.47:3,8,9.
The **peoples** will confess You, the **nations** will be glad and shout for joy, because You will judge the **peoples** with uprightness and will lead the **nations** on the earth. Ps.67:3,4.
Remember me, Jehovah, when You favour Your **people**, that I may rejoice in the joy of Your **nations**. Ps.106:4,5.
And other places too.

The reason why nations and peoples are mentioned together is that nations means those who are in possession of goodness, and in the opposite sense those in possession of evil, and peoples means those who are in possession of truths, and in the opposite sense those in possession of falsities. Therefore those who belong to the Lord's spiritual kingdom are called peoples, and those who belong to the Lord's celestial kingdom are called nations. For all who possess truths and the wisdom these provide are in the spiritual kingdom, whereas all who possess goodness and the love it brings are in the celestial kingdom.

87 It is similar with all other pairs of expressions, as for instance, when **Joy** is mentioned there is also a mention of **Gladness**, in the following places –

Behold, **joy** and **gladness**, the slaughtering of an ox. Isa.22:13.
They will obtain **joy** and **gladness**, and sorrow and groaning will flee away. Isa.35:10; 51:11.
Cut off from the house of our God is **gladness** and **joy**. Joel 1:16.
The voice of **joy** and the voice of **gladness** will be banished. Jer.7:34; 25:10.
The fast of the tenth month will become **joy** and **gladness** for the house of Judah. Zech.8:19.

Ut **gaudeamus** omnibus diebus nostris, **laetifica** nos. Ps.90:14,15.
Laetemini in Hierosolyma, **gaudete** in ea. Esai.66:10.
Gaude et **laetare**, filia Edomi. Thren.4:21.
Laetabuntur caeli et **gaudebit** terra. Ps.96:11.
5 Contra justi **laetabuntur**, et **gaudebunt in laetitia**. Ps.68:4.
Audire me facies **gaudium** et **laetitiam**. Ps.51:10.
Gaudium et **laetitia** invenietur in Zione, confessio et vox cantus. Esai.51:3.
Erit **laetitia**, et multi super nativitate Ipsius **gaudebunt**. Luc.1:14.
10 Cessare faciam vocem **gaudii** et vocem **laetitiae**, vocem sponsi et vocem sponsae. Jer.7:34; 16:9; 25:10.
Adhuc audietur in loco hoc vox **gaudii** et vox **laetitiae**, et vox sponsi et vox sponsae. Jer.33:10,11.
Et alibi.

15 Quod utrumque, tam gaudium quam laetitia, dicatur, est quia gaudium est boni et laetitia est veri, seu gaudium est amoris et laetitia est sapientiae, est enim gaudium cordis et laetitia animae, seu est gaudium voluntatis et laetitia intellectus. Quod conjugium Domini et ecclesiae etiam in his sit, patet ex
20 eo quod dicatur, Vox gaudii et vox laetitiae, vox sponsi et vox sponsae, Jer.7:34; 16:9; 25:10; 33:10,11; et Dominus est sponsus et ecclesia est sponsa. Quod Dominus sit sponsus, videatur, Matt.9:15; Marc.2:19,20; Luc.5:34,35; et quod ecclesia sit sponsa, Apoc.21:2,9; 22:17. Quare Johannes Baptista dicit de Jesu,

25 Qui habet sponsam sponsus est. Joh.3:29.

88 Propter conjugium Domini cum ecclesia seu, quod idem est, propter conjugium Divini Boni et Divini Veri, in singulis Verbi, permultis in locis dicitur Jehovah et Deus, ac Jehovah et Sanctus Israelis, sicut forent duo, cum tamen unum sunt, per
30 Jehovam enim intelligitur Dominus quoad Divinum Bonum, et per Deum, et per Sanctum Israelis Dominus quoad Divinum Verum. Quod Jehovah et Deus, tum Jehovah et Sanctus Israelis,

---

4-5 **Laetabuntur** caeli et **gaudebit** terra. Ps.96:11. Contra justi **laetabuntur, et gaudebunt in laetitia.** Ps.68:4: **Laetabuntur** caeli et **gaudebit** terra. Ps.68:4 SS^1, SS^2, VR^1, VR^2; Laetabuntur caeli et gaudebit terra. Ps.96:11 SS^3, VR^3
6 facies: facient SS, VR
31 et per Sanctum Israelis SS^3, VR: om SS^1, SS^2

That we may **rejoice** all our days, make us **glad**. Ps.90:14,15.
Be **glad** in Jerusalem, **rejoice** in her. Isa.66:10.
Rejoice and **be glad**, daughter of Edom. Lam.4:21.
The heavens will be **glad**, and the earth will **rejoice**. Ps.96:11.
On the other hand the upright will be **glad**, and will **rejoice in gladness**. Ps.68:3.
You will cause me to hear **joy** and **gladness**. Ps.51:8.
Joy and **gladness** will be found in Zion, confession and the sound of song. Isa.51:3.
There will be **gladness**, and many will **rejoice** over His birth. Luke 1:14.
I will cause to cease the voice of **joy** and the voice of **gladness**, the voice of the bridegroom and the voice of the bride. Jer.7:34; 16:9; 25:10.
There will still be heard in this place the voice of **joy** and the voice of **gladness**, and the voice of the bridegroom and the voice of the bride. Jer.33:10,11.
And other places.

The reason why both joy and gladness are mentioned is that joy refers to goodness and gladness to truth, or, joy refers to love and gladness to wisdom. For joy belongs to the heart and gladness to the soul, or, joy belongs to the will and gladness to the understanding. The existence of a marriage of the Lord and the church also in these is evident from the use, in Jer.7:34; 16:9; 25:10; 33:10,11, of the words, The voice of joy and the voice of gladness, the voice of the bridegroom and the voice of the bride, the Lord being the bridegroom and the church the bride. For the Lord as bridegroom, see Matt.9:15; Mark 2:19,20; Luke 5:34,35, and for the church as bride, Rev.21:2,9; 22:17. This is why John the Baptist says of Jesus, 2

He who has the bride is the bridegroom. John 3:29.

88 On account of the marriage of the Lord and the church or, what amounts to the same thing, the marriage of Divine Goodness and Divine Truth in the details of the Word, in very many places Jehovah and God, or Jehovah and the Holy One of Israel, are mentioned as if they were two, when in fact they are one. For Jehovah means the Lord in respect of Divine Goodness, and God and the Holy One of Israel mean the Lord in respect of Divine Truth. For the very many places in the Word where Jehovah and God, or Jehovah

in permultis locis in Verbo dicantur, et tamen intelligatur unus, qui est Dominus, in **Doctrina de Domino**, n.34,38,46, videatur.

89 Quoniam in omnibus et singulis Verbi est conjugium Domini et ecclesiae, constare potest quod omnia et singula Verbi de Domino agant, ut in **Doctrina de Domino**, n.1-7, caeptum est demonstrare. Ecclesia, de qua etiam agitur, est quoque Dominus, nam docet Dominus quod homo ecclesiae sit in Ipso et Ipse in illo, Joh.6:56; 14:20,21; 15:5,7.

90 Quia de Divinitate et Sanctitate Verbi hic agitur, aliquid memorabile illis quae hactenus dicta sunt adjicere licet. Quondam ad me e caelo missa est chartula exarata literis Hebraicis, sed scriptis sicut apud antiquos, apud quos illae literae quae hodie quoad aliquam partem lineares sunt, fuerunt inflexae cum corniculis sursum vergentibus. Et dicebant angeli qui tunc apud me erant, quod scirent integros sensus ex ipsis literis, et quod illos scirent imprimis ex flexuris linearum et apicum literae; et explicabant quid significarent seorsim et quid conjunctim, dicentes quod H, quod additum est nominibus Abrami et Sarai, significaret infinitum ac aeternum. Explicabant etiam coram me sensum Verbi, Ps.32:2, ex solis literis seu syllabis, quod sensus illarum in summa esset, *Quod Dominus etiam misericors sit illis qui malefaciunt.*

Informabant me quod scriptura in tertio caelo ex literis inflexis et varie incurvatis, quarum unaquaevis haberet sensum, constaret, et quod vocales ibi essent pro sono, qui correspondet affectioni, et quod in illo caelo non possent enuntiare vocales *i* et *e*, sed pro illis *y* et *eu*; et quod vocales *a, o*, et *u* illis in usu essent, quia dant sonum plenum. Tum quod non exprimerent aliquas literas consonantes aspere, sed molliter, et quod inde sit quod literae quaedam Hebraicae intus punctatae sint, in signum ut molliter enuntientur, dicentes quod asperitas in literis esset in usu in spirituali caelo, ex causa quia ibi in veris sunt, et verum admittit asperum, non autem bonum, in quo sunt angeli regni caelestis seu tertii caeli. Dicebant etiam quod Verbum apud se conscriptum haberent literis inflexis cum corniculis et apicibus significativis, ex quo patuit quid significant haec Domini,

and the Holy One of Israel, are mentioned when yet one is meant, that is, the Lord, see **Teaching concerning the Lord**, §§34,38,46.

89 Since every single detail of the Word contains the marriage of the Lord and the church, the Word in every detail has to do with the Lord, as was shown at the beginning of **Teaching concerning the Lord**, §§1-7. The church, which every detail also has to do with, is the Lord as well, for the Lord teaches that members of the church abide in Him and He in them, John 6:56; 14:20,21; 15:5,7.

90 Seeing that the Divinity and Holiness of the Word is the subject here let me add a certain experience to the things which have been mentioned so far.

Once a paper was sent to me from heaven written in Hebrew letters, but in the script used in ancient times; the letters which nowadays have in places straight lines were curved, with flourishes pointing upwards. The angels who were then present with me said that they gathered complete ideas from the letters themselves, knowing them especially from the curves of the lines and the serifs of the letters. They explained what these meant separately and what when combined. They said that H, which was added to the names of Abram and Sarai, meant what is infinite and eternal. They also explained in my presence the meaning of a verse of the Word, Ps.32:2, simply from the letters or characters; their meaning was in short, *That the Lord is merciful even to those who do wrong*.

They told me that writing in the third heaven consists of   2
letters bent into various curves, each of which possesses some meaning. Vowels there stood for the sound which corresponds to an affection. In that heaven they cannot pronounce the vowels *i* and *e*, but substitute for them *y* and *eu*[1]. They used the vowels *a*, *o*, and *u* because they give a full sound. They also said that they do not pronounce any consonants harshly, but softly; and this was why certain Hebrew letters have a point inside, as a sign they are pronounced softly. They said that harshness in letters was used in the spiritual heaven, because there they possess truths, and truth admits harshness, but goodness does not, and angels of the celestial kingdom, that is, the third heaven, possess goodness. They also said that they had among themselves the Word written in curved letters with flourishes and serifs which conveyed a meaning. This made it plain what these words of the Lord mean,

---

1 These letters must be understood as having values as in modern Italian, but *y* means the sound of French *u* or German *ü*

Non jotha et corniculum praeteribit de Lege, donec omnia fiunt. Matt.5:18;

tum,

Facilius est caelum et terram transire quam Legis unum apicem
5 cadere. Luc.16:17.

Not a jot nor a stroke will pass away from the Law until all things are done. Matt. 5:18.

Also,

It is easier for heaven and earth to pass away than for one dot of the Law to fall out. Luke 16:17.

Quod haereses ex sensu literae Verbi captari possint, sed quod confirmare illas damnosum sit

91   Supra ostensum est quod Verbum non possit intelligi absque doctrina, et quod doctrina sit sicut lucerna, ut genuina vera videantur; et hoc ex causa quia Verbum per meras correspondentias conscriptum est. Inde est quod plura ibi apparentiae veri sint et non nuda vera, et plura ad captum naturalis, imo sensualis, hominis scripta, sed tamen ita ut simplices illud simpliciter possint intelligere, et intelligentes intelligenter, ac sapientes sapienter. Nunc quia Verbum tale est, possunt apparentiae veri, quae sunt vestita vera, pro nudis veris captari, quae dum confirmantur fiunt falsa. Sed hoc fit ab illis qui supra alios se credunt sapere, cum tamen non sapiunt, nam sapere est videre num verum sit antequam confirmatur, non autem confirmare quodcunque lubet. Hoc faciunt illi qui genio confirmandi pollent, et in fastu propriae intelligentiae sunt, illud autem faciunt qui amant vera, et afficiuntur illis quia vera sunt, et faciunt illa usus vitae. Hi enim illustrantur a Domino ac vident vera ex luce illorum, illi autem illustrantur a semet et vident falsa etiam ex luce illorum.

92   Quod apparentiae veri, quae sunt vestita vera, pro nudis veris ex Verbo captari possint, et quod, dum confirmantur, fiant falsa, constare potest ex tot haeresibus quae in Christianismo fuerunt, et adhuc sunt. Ipsae haereses non damnant homines; sed vita mala, tum confirmationes falsitatum, quae in haeresi sunt, ex Verbo, et per ratiocinia ex naturali homine, damnant. Quisque enim nascitur in religionem parentum suorum, ab infantia initiatur in illam et postea retinet illam, nec potest semet ipsum educere ex falsis ejus propter negotia in mundo.

Heresies can be extracted from the literal sense of the Word but confirming them leads to damnation

91 It was demonstrated above that the Word cannot be understood without teaching, and that teaching resembles a lantern which allows genuine truths to be seen, and this is because the Word is entirely written by means of correspondences. That is why many things in it are appearances of truth and not bare truths, and why many things are written to be intelligible to people who are natural, that is, think on the level of the senses, yet in such a way that the simple can understand it simply, the intelligent intelligently, and the wise wisely. Seeing that the Word is like this the appearances of truth, which are clothed truths, can be taken for bare truths; and when these are confirmed they become falsities. But this happens in the case of those who think they are wiser than others, though in fact they are not wise, for being wise consists in first seeing whether something really is the truth before confirming it, not in confirming whatever you like. The latter is what people do who are well able to confirm things and who arrogantly trust their own intelligence, whereas the former is what other people do who love truths and are moved by them because they are truths, and who put them to use in life. Such people are enlightened by the Lord and see truths in the light of these, whereas the former are enlightened by self and see falsities in the light of these.

92 The fact that the appearances of truth, which are clothed truths, can be taken to be bare truths derived from the Word, and that when they are confirmed they become falsities, becomes clear from so many heresies that have existed in Christianity, and still do. It is not the heresies themselves that damn people; rather it is an evil life together with the confirmations from the Word of falsities contained in heresy and the reasonings springing from the natural level of the human mind that damn them. For everyone by birth acquires their religion from their parents. From early childhood they are introduced to it and afterwards retain it; nor can they extricate themselves from its falsities on account of their attention to business

Sed vivere male et confirmare falsa usque ad destructionem genuini veri, hoc damnat. Nam qui manet in sua religione et credit in Deum, ac intra Christianismum credit in Dominum, et Verbum sanctum habet, et secundum praecepta Decalogi ex religione vivit, is non jurat in falsa; quare dum audit vera et suo modo percipit illa, potest illa amplecti et sic a falsis educi. Non autem ille qui falsa religionis suae confirmaverat, nam falsum confirmatum manet et non potest exstirpari, est enim falsum post confirmationem, sicut quis juraverit in illud, imprimis si cohaeret cum amore proprii et inde fastu sapientiae.

93 Loquutus sum cum quibusdam in mundo spirituali qui ante plura saecula vixerunt et se confirmaverunt in falsis religionis suae, et compertus sum quod in iisdem adhuc constanter manerent. Et loquutus sum cum quibusdam ibi qui ex eadem religione fuerunt et cogitaverunt sicut illi sed non confirmaverunt falsa ejus apud se, et compertus sum quod instructi ab angelis falsa rejecerint et vera imbuerint, et quod hi salvati sint, non autem illi. Unusquisque homo post mortem instruitur ab angelis, et recipiuntur illi qui vera vident et ex veris falsa, nam datur cuivis vera spiritualiter videre post mortem. Vera vident illi qui non se confirmaverunt in falsis, sed qui se confirmaverunt, non volunt videre vera; et si vident, se retro vertunt, et tunc vel ad illa rident vel illa falsificant.

94 Sed hoc illustretur per exemplum. In Verbo multis in locis tribuitur Domino ira, excandescentia, vindicta, et quod puniat, dejiciat in infernum, tentet, et plura similia. Qui hoc simpliciter credit, et propterea timet Deum, et sibi cavet a peccare contra Ipsum, ille propter simplicem illam fidem non damnatur. Sed qui apud se confirmat illa eousque ut credat quod ira, excandescentia, vindicta, et sic talia quae mali sunt, apud Dominum sint, et quod ex ira, excandescentia, et vindicta hominem puniat et in infernum dejiciat, ille damnatur, quia genuinum verum destruxit, quod est quod Dominus sit ipse Amor, ipsa Misericordia, et ipsum Bonum, et qui est illa, non potest irasci, excandescere, et vindicare. Quod illa Domino tribuantur, est ex apparentia. Similiter in multis aliis.

21 in falsis SS^3: om SS^1, SS^2

in the world. But leading a wicked life and confirming falsities to the point that genuine truth is destroyed, this is what brings damnation. For people who stay with their religion and believe in God, and within Christianity believe in the Lord, regard the Word as holy, and live for religious reasons according to the Ten Commandments – they do not swear allegiance to falsities. So when they hear truths and perceive them in their own fashion they can embrace them and so be led away from falsities. But this is not the case with people who have confirmed the falsities taught by their religion, because falsity once confirmed remains and cannot be rooted out. For, when it has been confirmed, falsity is as if people have sworn allegiance to it, especially if it has stuck fast to their love of self and consequent pride in their own wisdom.

93 I have spoken to some people in the spiritual world who lived many centuries ago and convinced themselves of the falsities taught by their religion, and I learned that they still steadfastly remain convinced by them. And I have spoken to some there who belonged to the same religion and had thought just as the others but had not confirmed the falsities in their minds, and I learned that these under instruction by angels have rejected falsities and adopted truths. These have been saved, but not the others. After death everyone is instructed by angels, and those are accepted who see truths, and falsities in the light of truths, for anyone is allowed after death to see truths on a spiritual level. But the only ones who do see them are those who have not convinced themselves of falsities; those who have convinced themselves of them are not willing to see them; and if they do, they turn away and then either laugh at them or turn them into falsities.

94 But let an example be given to illustrate this. In many places in the Word anger, wrath, and vengeance are attributed to the Lord, and He is said to punish, cast into hell, tempt, and so on. People who believe this in their simplicity, and who therefore fear God and take care not to sin against Him, are not damned for having that simple belief. But if people so convince themselves of these things as to believe that anger, wrath, vengeance, and so actions characteristic of a wicked person can be attributed to the Lord, and that in anger, wrath, and vengeance He punishes and casts a person into hell, they are damned for destroying a genuine truth. This is that the Lord is Love itself, Mercy itself, and Goodness itself, and one who is all these cannot be angry, wrathful, and demand vengeance. The latter are attributed to the Lord because it is how He appears to be. The like applies in many other cases.

DOCTRINA DE SCRIPTURA SACRA

95 Quod plura in sensu literae sint vera apparentia in quibus vera genuina latent, et quod non damnosum sit secundum vera apparentia cogitare et loqui, sed quod damnosum sit confirmare illa usque ad destructionem genuini veri quod intus latet, illustrari etiam potest per exemplum in natura, quod adfertur, quia naturale clarius quam spirituale docet et persuadet. Coram oculis apparet sicut sol quovis die circum tellurem feratur, et quoque semel quotannis; inde in Verbo dicitur quod sol oriatur et occidat, quod faciat mane, meridiem, vesperam, et noctem, atque tempora veris, aestatis, autumni, et hyemis, et sic dies et annos, cum tamen sol immotus stat, est enim oceanus igneus et tellus circumvolvitur quotidie et circumfertur quotannis. Homo qui ex simplicitate et ex ignorantia cogitat quod circumferatur, non destruit veritatem naturalem, quae est quod tellus quotidie rotetur circum axem, et quotannis feratur secundum eclipticam. At qui confirmat apparentem solis motum et cursum per Verbum, et per ratiocinia ex naturali homine, is infirmat veritatem et quoque destruit illam.

Quod sol moveatur est apparens verum, quod non moveatur est genuinum verum. Quisque potest loqui secundum apparens verum, et quoque loquitur, sed cogitare secundum illud ex confirmatione, hoc intellectum rationalem hebetat et opacat. Simile est cum stellis caeli astriferi. Apparens verum est quod illae quoque semel quotidie, sicut sol, circumferantur, quare dicitur etiam de stellis quod oriantur et occidant. Sed genuinum verum est quod stellae sint fixae, et quod caelum illarum immotum stet. Attamen potest quisque secundum apparentiam loqui.

96 Quod damnosum sit confirmare apparens verum Verbi, usque ad destructionem genuini veri quod intus latet, est quia omnia et singula sensus literae Verbi communicant cum caelo et aperiunt illud, secundum illa quae supra, n.62-69, dicta sunt. Cum itaque homo illum sensum applicat ad confirmandum amores mundi contrarios amoribus caeli, tunc internum Verbi falsum fit. Quare cum externum ejus, quod est sensus literae, cujus internum est falsum, communicatur cum caelo, tunc clauditur caelum, nam angeli, qui in interno Verbi

---

3   vera apparentia: vera SS^1, SS^2; talia vera SS^3; apparentias veri VR

95	An example from nature may serve to illustrate that many things in the literal sense are apparent truths, in which genuine truths are hidden, and that it is not injurious to think and to speak according to apparent truths, but that it is injurious to confirm them so much as to destroy the genuine truth hidden within them. This example is offered because what is natural provides an easier way than what is spiritual to inform and be convincing.

[2] It appears to the eyes that the sun travels round the earth every day and also once every year. The Word therefore speaks of the sun rising and setting, causing morning, noon, evening, and night, and the seasons of spring, summer, autumn, and winter, thus days and years. Yet the sun stands unmoved, for it is a sea of fire, and it is the earth which rotates every day and travels around its orbit every year. People who in simplicity or in ignorance think that it travels round the earth do not destroy the natural truth, which is that the earth every day rotates on its axis and every year travels around the ecliptic. But if people through the Word and the reasonings of the natural mind convince themselves of the sun's apparent motion and journeying they weaken the truth and even destroy it.

[3] The movement of the sun is an apparent truth, its not moving is a genuine truth. Everyone may speak, indeed does speak, according to the apparent truth; but to think according to it after confirming it blunts and dulls the rational understanding. Similarly so with the stars in the sky. The apparent truth is that these too travel round once every day like the sun, and therefore it is said of the stars also that they rise and set. But the genuine truth is that the stars are fixed and that the sky stands unmoved. Yet everyone may speak according to the appearance.

96	The reason why it is injurious to confirm an apparent truth in the Word, so much as to destroy the genuine truth hidden within it, is that every detail of the literal sense of the Word communicates with heaven and opens it up, in accord with what has been stated above, in §§62-69. When therefore people use that sense in support of worldly desires that are the opposite of heavenly ones the inward content of the Word is rendered false. Consequently when the outward content of it, that is, the literal sense, whose inward content is false, communicates with heaven, heaven is shut off, because it is rejected by the angels, with whom the inward content exists. From

sunt, rejiciunt illud. Ex quo patet quod falsum internum seu verum falsificatum auferat communicationem cum caelo et claudat illud. Haec causa est quod confirmare aliquod falsum haereticum damnosum sit.

96a Verbum est sicut hortus, qui paradisus caelestis vocandus est, in quo cupediae et delitiae omnis generis sunt – cupediae ex fructibus et delitiae ex floribus – in cujus medio sunt arbores vitae, juxta quas fontes aquae vivae; at circumcirca hortum sunt arbores sylvae. Homo qui ex doctrina in Divinis veris est in medio est, ubi sunt arbores vitae, et actualiter cupediis et delitiis inde fruitur. Homo autem qui non ex doctrina in veris est sed ex solo sensu literae, is in circuitu est et videt modo sylvestria. At qui in doctrina religionis falsae est et falsum ejus apud se confirmavit, ne quidem in sylva est sed extra illam in campo arenoso ubi nec gramen. Quod etiam talis status illorum post mortem sit, in suo loco confirmabitur.

97 Insuper sciendum est quod sensus literae Verbi sit custodia pro genuinis veris quae intus latent; et in eo est custodia, quod ille sensus possit huc illuc verti, et explicari secundum captum, et per id tamen internum non laedi et violari. Non enim nocet ut sensus literae Verbi aliter ab uno quam ab altero intelligatur, sed id nocet si Divina vera quae intus latent pervertantur, per hoc enim infertur Verbo violentia. Ne hoc fiat, custodit sensus literae, et custodit apud illos qui in falsis sunt ex religione et falsa illa non confirmant, nam hi non aliquam violentiam inferunt.

Haec custodia significatur per cherubos, et quoque describitur per illos in Verbo. Illa significatur per cherubos qui, postquam Adamus cum uxore ejectus est ex horto Edenis, ad introitum ejus positi sunt, de quibus haec leguntur,

Cum Jehovah Deus expulerat hominem, habitare fecit ab oriente horti Edenis cherubos, et flammam gladii hinc inde vertentis se, ad custodiendum viam arboris vitae. Gen.3:23,24.

---

16   talis ... sit SS^2, *VR*: tales ... sit SS^1; tales ... sint SS^3

this it is plain that the false inward content or falsified truth breaks the communication with heaven and shuts it off. This is why it is injurious to confirm any heretical falsity.

96a[1] The Word is like a garden, which may be called the heavenly paradise, containing dainties and delights of every kind – the dainties consisting of fruits and the delights of flowers. In the midst of it there are the trees of life growing hard by springs of living water; but surrounding the garden there are woodland trees. People who are in possession of Divine truths obtained from teaching are in the middle, where the trees of life are, and in fact they enjoy the dainties and delights from there. People in possession of truths obtained not from teaching but solely from the literal sense are on the circumference and see only the woodland. But those who possess the teaching belonging to a false religion and have convinced themselves of the falsity it contains are not even in the wood but outside it in a sandy plain where there is no grass either. Corroboration that such is the condition of these people after death will be seen in a place of its own.

97 It should furthermore be known that the literal sense of the Word serves to protect the genuine truths hidden within. It does so because that sense can be twisted in different directions and explained as it is understood without what is within being harmed or violated. For it does no harm for the literal sense of the Word to be understood differently by different people, but harm is done if the Divine truths hidden within are distorted. This is what does violence to the Word. The literal sense acts as a protection to prevent this from happening, and this occurs with those whose religion has given them false ideas but who have not convinced themselves of these falsities, for such people are not doing violence.

This protection is meant by the cherubim, and is also [2] described by them in the Word. It is meant by the cherubim which were placed at the entrance to the garden of Eden after Adam and his wife were expelled from it. We read of these,

When Jehovah God had cast out the man He caused cherubim to dwell on the east of the garden of Eden, and the flame of a sword turning this way and that, to protect the way to the tree of life. Gen.3:23,24.

---

1   In the first Latin edition this paragraph and the previous one are both numbered 96

Per cherubos significatur custodia; per viam arboris vitae significatur introitus ad Dominum, qui hominibus est per Verbum; per flammam gladii hinc inde vertentis se significatur Divinum Verum in ultimis, quod est sicut Verbum in sensu literae, qui ita verti potest.

Simile intelligitur per cherubos ex auro positos super duabus extremitatibus propitiatorii, quod erat super arca in tabernaculo, Exod.25:18-21. Quia hoc significabatur per cherubos, ideo Dominus inter illos loquutus est cum Mose, Exod.25:22; 37:9; Num.7:89. Quod Dominus loquatur cum homine non nisi quam in pleno et Verbum in sensu literae est Divinum Verum in pleno, videatur supra, n.37-49, sic itaque Dominus loquutus est cum Mose inter cherubos. Nec aliud significatum est per cherubos super aulaeis tabernaculi et super velo ibi, Exod.26:1,31; nam aulaea et vela tabernaculi repraesentabant ultima caeli et ecclesiae, ac ita etiam Verbi, videatur supra, n.46. Nec aliud significatum est per cherubos in medio templi Hierosolymitani, 1 Reg.6:23-28, et per cherubos sculptos super parietibus et super foribus templi, 1 Reg.6:29,32,35, similiter per cherubos in novo templo, Ezech.41:18-20, videatur etiam supra, n.47.

Quoniam per cherubos significabatur custodia ne Dominus, caelum, et Divinum Verum, quale est intus in Verbo, immediate adeantur, sed mediate per ultima, ideo de Rege Tyri ita dicitur,

Tu obsignans demensum, plenus sapientia et perfectus pulchritudine, in Eden horto fuisti; omnis lapis pretiosus tegumentum tuum. Tu, cherube, expansio contegentis. Perdidi te, cherube contegens, in medio lapidum ignis. Ezech.28:12-14,16.

Per Tyrum significatur ecclesia quoad cognitiones veri et boni, et inde per regem ejus Verbum ubi et unde cognitiones illae sunt. Quod Verbum hic in suo ultimo, quod est sensus literae, per illum, et per cherubum custodia, significetur, patet, nam dicitur,Tu obsignans demensum; omnis lapis pretiosus tegumentum tuum; ac tu, cherube, expansio contegentis; ut et cherube contegens. Quod per lapides pretiosos, qui etiam ibi nominantur, intelligantur vera sensus literae Verbi, videatur supra, n.45.

The cherubim mean protection; the way to the tree of life means the approach to the Lord, which people make by means of the Word; the flame of a sword turning this way and that means Divine Truth at the outermost level, which resembles the Word in its literal sense, in being capable of being twisted like this.

3 The meaning of the cherubim made of gold placed on the two ends of the mercy-seat, which was above the ark in the tabernacle, Exod.25:18-21, is similar. It was because the cherubim had that meaning that the Lord spoke to Moses from between them, Exod.25:22; 37:9; Num.7:89. The Lord does not speak to people except in fullness, and the Word in the literal sense is Divine Truth in fullness, see above, §§37-49, which being so the Lord spoke to Moses from between the cherubim. Nor was anything else meant by the cherubim on the hangings of the tabernacle and on the veil there, Exod.26:1,31, for the hangings and veils of the tabernacle represented the outermost parts of heaven and the church, and so also of the Word, see §46 above. Nothing else was meant, either, by the cherubim inside the temple in Jerusalem, 1 Kings 6:23-28, and by the cherubim carved on the walls and the doors of the temple, 1 Kings 6:29,32,35, likewise the cherubim in the new temple, Ezek.41:18-20, see also §47 above.

4 It was because cherubim served to mean protection which guarded against direct approach to the Lord, heaven, and Divine Truth as it exists on the inward levels of the Word – though indirect approach was allowable through its outermost levels – that the following is said about the king of Tyre,

You who set your seal on your measured space, full of wisdom and perfect in beauty. You were in the garden of Eden; every kind of precious stone was your covering. You, cherub, were the expanse of the covering. I have destroyed you, cherub who cover, in the midst of the stones of fire. Ezek.28:12-14,16.

Tyre means the church as regards its knowledge of truth and goodness, and so its king means the Word, which is the place and source of that knowledge. It is obvious that in these verses he means the Word at the outermost level, that is, the literal sense, and that cherub means protection, for it says, You who set your seal on your measured space; every kind of precious stone was your covering; and, You, cherub, were the expanse of the covering; as well as, Cherub who cover. The precious stones which are also named there mean the truths of the literal sense of the Word, see §45 above.

Quoniam per cherubos significatur ultimum Divini Veri, ut et custodia, ideo dicitur apud Davidem,

Jehovah inclinavit caelos et descendit, et equitavit super cherubo. Ps18:10,11.
Pastor Israelis, qui sedes super cherubis, effulge. Ps.80:2.
Jehovah insidens cherubis. Ps.99:1.

Equitare super cherubis, sedere super illis, et insidere illis est super sensu ultimo Verbi. Divinum Verum in Verbo, et ejus quale, describitur per cherubos apud Ezechielem, in capite primo, et in nono, et decimo; et quia nemo scire potest quid per singula descriptionis illorum significatur nisi cui apertus est sensus spiritualis, ideo mihi detectum est quid in summa per omnia illa quae de cherubis dicuntur in primo capite apud Ezechielem, significatur, quae haec sunt –

Describitur Divina sphaera externa Verbi, vers.4; illa repraesentata sicut homo, vers.5; conjuncta spiritualibus et caelestibus, vers.6; naturale Verbi, quale est, vers.7; spirituale et caeleste Verbi conjunctum naturali ejus, quale, vers.8,9; Divinus Amor boni et veri caelestis, spiritualis, et naturalis inibi, distinctim, et simul, vers.10,11; quod ad unum spectent, vers.12; sphaera Verbi ex Divino Bono et Divino Vero Domini, ex quibus Verbum vivit, vers.13,14; doctrina boni et veri in Verbo et ex Verbo, vers.15-21; Divinum Domini supra illud et in illo, vers.22,23; et ex illo, vers.24,25; quod Dominus sit supra caelos, vers.26; et quod Ipsi sit Divinus Amor et Divina Sapientia, vers.27,28.

Haec summaria etiam collata sunt cum Verbo in caelo, et cum illo conformia sunt.

---

2   ut et: ut *AR, SS*; et quoque *VR*
5   sedes: sedet *AR, SS, VR*
10 et quia *AR*: at quia *SS*

TEACHING CONCERNING SACRED SCRIPTURE n.97

Because cherubim mean the outermost level of Divine Truth and also its protection, it says in David,

Jehovah bowed the heavens and came down, and rode upon a cherub. Ps.18:9.10.
O Shepherd of Israel, You who are seated on the cherubim, shine forth. Ps.80:1.
Jehovah that sits upon the cherubim. Ps.99:1.

Riding upon the cherubim, seated on them, and sitting upon them means upon the outermost sense of the Word. The Divine Truth in the Word and its nature are described by the cherubim in Ezekiel, in chapters 1, 9, and 10. But since none can know what the details describing them mean unless the spiritual sense is opened up for them, it has therefore been revealed to me what all those things said in the first chapter of Ezekiel about the cherubim mean briefly, namely this –

The outward Divine sphere of the Word is described, verse 4. This sphere is represented as a human being, verse 5. It is linked to things spiritual and celestial, verse 6. What the natural level of the Word is like, verse 7. What the spiritual and celestial levels of the Word linked to its natural are like, verses 8,9. The Divine Love within the Word resides simultaneously in distinct and separate levels of celestial, spiritual, and natural goodness and truth, verses 10,11. They look to one end, verse 12. The sphere of the Word emanating from the Lord's Divine Goodness and Divine Truth, by which the Word is made living, verses 13,14. Teaching of what is good and true present in the Word and obtained from the Word, verses 15-21. The Lord's Divinity is above it and within it, verses 22,23, and coming from it, verses 24,25. The Lord is above the heavens, verse 26. And to Him belong Divine Love and Divine Wisdom, verses 27,28.

These brief explanations have also been placed alongside the Word in heaven and have been in agreement with it.[1]

---

1 The wording in this brief explanation of the first chapter of Ezekiel is virtually the same as that contained in a manuscript, found among Swedenborg's possessions after his death, that presents briefly the inner meaning of the OT Books Isaiah-Malachi, and all the Psalms. Regarding this manuscript, see page ix of the Editor and Translator's Introduction to **Doctrina Novae Hierosolymae de Domino (DD)** – published in 2019 – under the subheading *Prophets and Psalms*

Quod Dominus in mundum venerit ut impleret omnia Verbi, et per id fieret Divinum Verum seu Verbum etiam in ultimis

98 Quod Dominus in mundum venerit ut impleret omnia Verbi, videatur in **Doctrina de Domino**, n.8-11. Quod per id factus sit Divinum Verum seu Verbum etiam in ultimis, intelligitur per haec apud Johannem,

Verbum caro factum est, et habitavit inter nos, et vidimus gloriam Ipsius, gloriam sicut unigeniti a Patre, plenus gratia et veritate. 1:14.

Fieri caro est fieri Verbum in ultimis. Qualis fuit ut Verbum in ultimis, ostendit discipulis cum transformatus est, Matt.17:2, seq.; Marc.9:2, seq.; Luc.9:28 seq.; et ibi dicitur quod Moses et Elias visi sint in gloria; per Mosen et Eliam intelligitur Verbum, videatur supra, n.48. Dominus ut Verbum in ultimis, etiam describitur apud Johannem in Apocalypsi 1:13-16, ubi omnia descriptionis Ipsius significant ultima Divini Veri seu Verbi. Dominus prius quidem fuerat Verbum, sed in primis, nam dicitur,

In principio erat Verbum, et Verbum erat apud Deum, et Deus erat Verbum. Hoc erat in principio apud Deum. Joh.1:1-3.

Sed quando Verbum caro factum est, tunc Dominus factus est Verbum etiam in ultimis. Ex eo est quod dicatur, Primus et Ultimus, Apoc.1:8,11,17; 2:8; 21:6; 22:12,13.

99 Per id quod Dominus etiam factus sit Verbum in ultimis, status ecclesiae prorsus mutatus est. Omnes ecclesiae quae ante adventum Ipsius fuerunt, ecclesiae representativae fuerunt, quae Divinum Verum non videre potuerunt nisi quam in umbra. At post adventum Domini in mundum ecclesia ab Ipso instituta est quae Divinum Verum vidit in luce. Differentia est, qualis inter vesperam et mane; status ecclesiae ante adventum Ipsius etiam vocatur Vespera, et

The Lord came into the world to fulfil everything in the Word and in doing so He became Divine Truth, that is, the Word even in its outermost form

98   Regarding the Lord's coming into the world to fulfil everything in the Word, see **Teaching concerning the Lord**, §§8-11. In doing so He became Divine Truth, that is, the Word even in its outermost form, and this is what is meant by these words in John,

The Word was made flesh and dwelt among us, and we saw His glory, glory as of the only-begotten of the Father, full of grace and truth. 1:14.

Being made flesh is becoming the Word in its outermost form. He showed the disciples, when He was transfigured, what the Word was like in its outermost form, Matt.17:2 and following verses; Mark 9:2 and following verses; Luke 9:28 and following verses. And in these places it says that Moses and Elijah were seen in glory; Moses and Elijah mean the Word, see above, §48. The Lord as the Word in outermost form is also described by John, in Rev.1:13-16. There all the details describing Him mean the outermost form of Divine Truth, that is, the Word. The Lord had indeed previously been the Word, but in its first beginnings, for it says,

In the beginning was the Word, and the Word was with God, and the Word was God. The same was in the beginning with God. John 1:1-3.

But when the Word was made flesh, then the Lord became the Word even in its outermost form. This is why He is called the First and the Last, Rev.1:8,11,17; 2:8; 21:6; 22:12,13.

99   Because the Lord became the Word even in its outermost form, the state of the church was completely altered. All the churches that existed before He came were representative churches, which were unable to see Divine Truth except in shadow. But after He came into the world a church was established by Him which saw Divine Truth in bright light. The difference is like that between evening and morning; indeed the condition of the church before His

status ecclesiae post adventum Ipsius vocatur Mane. Dominus ante adventum Suum in mundum quidem praesens fuit apud homines ecclesiae, sed mediate per caelum, at post adventum Suum in mundum praesens est apud homines ecclesiae immediate, nam in mundo induit etiam Divinum Naturale, in quo apud homines praesens est. Glorificatio Domini est glorificatio Humani Ipsius quod assumsit in mundo, ac Humanum Domini glorificatum est Divinum Naturale.

100 Quomodo Dominus est Verbum, a paucis intelligitur, cogitant enim quod Dominus quidem per Verbum possit hominem illustrare et docere, et tamen non inde potest vocari Verbum. At sciant quod unusquisque homo sit suus amor, et inde suum bonum et suum verum; homo non aliunde est homo, et non aliud apud illum est homo. Ex eo quod homo sit suum bonum et suum verum, sunt etiam angeli et spiritus homines, nam omne bonum et verum procedens a Domino in sua forma est homo. Dominus autem est ipsum Divinum Bonum et Divinum Verum, ita est ipse Homo, a quo omnis homo est homo. Quod omne Divinum Bonum et Divinum Verum in sua forma sit Homo, videatur in opere **De Caelo et Inferno**, n.460, et clarius videbitur in transactionibus sequentibus, quae erunt de **Sapientia Angelica**.

---

10 possit *VR*: potest *SS*

coming is called Evening, and the condition of the church after His coming is called Morning. Before the Lord came into the world He was, it is true, present with members of the church, but only indirectly through heaven, whereas after His coming into the world He has been present with members of the church directly. This is so because in the world He has taken on the Divine Natural as well in which He is present with people. The glorification of the Lord is the glorification of His Human which He adopted in the world, and the Lord's glorified Human is the Divine Natural.

100   Few people understand how it is that the Lord is the Word. For they consider that though the Lord can by means of the Word illuminate and teach a person, He cannot for this reason be called the Word. But they should know that every individual person is their own love, and consequently their own goodness and their own truth. This is the only thing that makes them a human being, and being a human being consists in nothing else. And for the same reason that a human being is their own goodness and their own truth, angels and spirits are human, for all goodness and truth emanating from the Lord is, in its own form, human. The Lord however is Divine Goodness and Divine Truth themselves, and so is Humanity itself, from whom every person is human. That all Divine Goodness and Divine Truth are in their own form Human may be seen in the work **Heaven and Hell**, §460, and will be seen more clearly in publications to follow which will be dealing with **Angelic Wisdom**.[1]

---

1   See, in Swedenborg's Preface to **Doctrina Novae Hierosolymae de Domino (DD)**, the last four of the subjects he was intending to deal with in forthcoming publications

Quod ante hoc Verbum quod hodie est in mundo fuerit Verbum quod deperditum est

101 Quod ante Verbum per Mosen et Prophetas apud gentem Israeliticam datum, cultus per sacrificia notus fuerit, et quod ex ore Jehovae prophetaverint, ex memoratis in Libris Mosis constare potest. *Quod cultus per sacrificia notus fuerit*, ex his: Mandatum est ut filii Israelis gentium altaria everterent, illarum statuas confringerent, et illarum lucos exscinderent, Exod.34:13; Deut.7:5; 12:3. Quod Israel in Schittim caeperit scortari cum filiabus Moabi, quod vocaverint populum ad sacrificia deorum suorum, et quod comederit populus, et incurvaverit se diis eorum, et imprimis adjunxerit se Baalpeori; et quod accensa sit ira Jehovae contra Israelem propterea, Num.25:1-3. Tum quod Bileamus, qui fuit ex Syria, fecerit exstruere altaria, et sacrificaverit boves et pecudes, Num.22:40; 23:1,2,14,29. *Quod etiam ex ore Jehovae prophetaverint*, constat ex Prophetiis Bileami, Num.23:7-10,18-24; 24:3-9,16-24. Quod etiam prophetaverit de Domino, quod oriretur stella ex Jacobo, et sceptrum ex Israele, Num.24:17. Quod prophetaverit ex ore Jehovae, Num.22:13,18; 23:3,5,8,16,26; 24:1,13. Ex his patet quod cultus Divinus similis cultui apud gentem Israeliticam per Mosen instituto apud gentes fuerit.

Quod etiam ante Abrami tempus fuerit, aliquantum elucet ex verbis apud Mosen, Deut.32:7,8; sed evidentius ex Malchizedecho rege Schalemi, Quod eduxerit panem et vinum, et benedixerit Abramo, et quod Abram dederit ei decimas de omnibus, Gen.14:18-20; et quod Malchizedech repraesentaverit Dominum, nam vocatur Sacerdos Deo Altissimo, Gen.14:18; et de Domino dicitur apud Davidem, Tu Sacerdos in aeternum, juxta modum Malchizedechi, Ps.110:4. Inde erat quod Malchizedech eduxerit panem et vinum ut

---

10 quod SS^3,VR^3: *om* SS^1, SS^2, VR^1, VR^2
11 quod SS^3,VR: *om* SS^1, SS^2

Before the time of the Word which exists in the world today there was another Word now lost

101 It becomes clear from what is recorded in the books of Moses that before the time of the Word which was given to the Israelite nation through Moses and the Prophets, worship by sacrifices was well known, and that prophecies were given from the mouth of Jehovah. The fact that *worship by sacrifices was well known* is evident from the following places: The children of Israel were commanded to overturn the altars of the nations,[1] break in pieces their statues, and cut down their sacred groves, Exod.34:13; Deut.7:5; 12:3. Israel in Shittim began to behave promiscuously with the daughters of Moab, who invited the people to the sacrifices of their gods. The people ate and bowed down to their gods, and associated themselves in particular with Baal of Peor; and Jehovah's anger was kindled against Israel because of this, Num.25:1-3. Also, Balaam, who came from Syria, had altars built and sacrificed cattle and sheep, Num.22:40; 23:1,2,14,29,30. And the fact that *prophecies were given from the mouth of Jehovah* is clear from Balaam's prophetic utterances, Num.23:7-10,18-24; 24:3-9,16-24. He also prophesied about the Lord, that a star would arise from Jacob and a sceptre from Israel, Num.24:17. He gave prophecies from the mouth of Jehovah, Num.22:13,18; 23:3,5,8,16,26; 24:1,13. It is plain from all this that the nations had Divine worship like that established for the Israelite nation through Moses. Also, the fact that *it existed even before the time of Abram* is made fairly plain by the words used in Moses at Deut.32:7,8, but it is even more obvious from the case of Melchizedek, king of Salem. He brought out bread and wine, and blessed Abram; and Abram gave him tithes of everything, Gen.14:18-20. Melchizedek represented the Lord, for he is called the priest of God Most High, Gen.14:18, and it is said of the Lord in David, You are a priest for ever after the fashion of Melchizedek, Ps.110:4. This was why Melchizedek brought out bread and wine as

---

1 ie the nations occupying Canaan, the promised land

sancta ecclesiae, sicut in Sacramento Caenae sancta sunt; et quod Malchizedech potuerit benedicere Abramo, et quod Abram dederit ei decimas de omnibus.

102 Quod Verbum apud antiquos fuerit conscriptum per meras correspondentias sed quod deperditum sit, relatum mihi est per angelos caeli; et dictum quod id Verbum adhuc apud illos conservatum sit, et in usu apud antiquos in illo caelo apud quos, cum in mundo fuerunt, id Verbum fuit. Antiqui illi apud quos illud Verbum in caelo adhuc in usu est fuerunt quoad partem ex terra Canaane, et ex confiniis ejus, ut ex Syria, Mesopotamia, Arabia, Chaldaea, Assyria, ex Aegypto, ex Zidone, Tyro, et Ninive, quorum omnium regnorum incolae fuerunt in cultu repraesentativo, et inde in scientia correspondentiarum. Sapientia illius temporis fuit ex illa scientia, et per illam fuit illis perceptio interior, et communicatio cum caelis. Illi qui correspondentias istius Verbi interius noverunt vocati sunt sapientes et intelligentes, at postea divinatores et magi.

Sed quia id Verbum erat plenum talibus correspondentiis quae remote significabant caelestia et spiritualia, et inde a multis incepit falsificari, ideo ex Divina Domini Providentia id successu temporis evanuit et tandem deperditum est, et aliud Verbum, per correspondentias non ita remotas conscriptum, datum est, et hoc per Prophetas apud filios Israelis. In hoc tamen Verbo retenta sunt plura nomina locorum quae in terra Canaane ac circum circa in Asia sunt, in quo significant similia quae in Verbo vetusto. Propter hanc causam Abram in illam terram ire jussus est, et ejus posteri ex Jacobo in illam introducti sunt.

103 Quod Verbum apud antiquos fuerit, constat etiam apud Mosen, a quo nominatur et aliquod desumptum est, Num.21:14,15,27-30; et quod historica illius Verbi appellata sint **Bella Jehovae**, ac prophetica **Enuntiata**. Ex historicis istius Verbi a Mose desumptum est hoc,

being the holy things of the church, just as they are the holy things in the Sacrament of the Lord's Supper, and why Melchizedek was able to bless Abram, and Abram gave him tithes of everything.

102   A Word existed, angels of heaven have told me, among ancient peoples which was composed of nothing else than correspondences, but which is now lost. They said that this Word has been preserved even until now among those ancient peoples, and that it is in use in the heaven among whose inhabitants that Word existed when they were in the world. These ancient peoples with whom that Word is still in use in heaven came in part from the land of Canaan and bordering regions, that is, Syria, Mesopotamia, Arabia, Chaldaea, Assyria, Egypt, Sidon, Tyre, and Nineveh. The worship of those inhabiting all these regions was representative, which means that those people were in possession of the knowledge of correspondences. The wisdom of those times lay in that knowledge, and through it those people were inwardly perceptive and in communication with the heavens. Those who had an inner knowledge of the correspondences in that Word were called the wise and intelligent, but later on sorcerers and magicians.[1]

But because that Word was full of the kinds of correspondences which stood at a remove to mean celestial and spiritual realities, and from those correspondences many began to falsify it, it consequently disappeared, in the Lord's Divine providence, as time went by and at length became lost. Then another Word was provided in which correspondences at less a remove were used in the composition of it; it was provided through the prophets among the children of Israel. However, quite a number of names of places in the land of Canaan and round about in Asia were retained in this Word, in which things carried a similar meaning to those in the old Word. It was for this reason that Abram was commanded to go to that land, and his descendants through Jacob were brought into it.

103   The existence of a Word among ancient peoples is also evident in the books of Moses, who refers to it and quotes from it, Num.21:14,15,27-30. The historical parts of that Word were called **The Wars of Jehovah**, and the prophetical parts **The Utterances**. The following is a quotation taken by Moses from the historical parts of that Word,

---

1   The Latin word *magi* (Greek *magoi*) was used sometimes to mean those who applied their knowledge of spiritual signs and symbols correctly and wisely, at other times to mean those who were practitioners of the occult

Propterea dicitur in **Libro Bellorum Jehovae**, Vahebam in Supha, et fluvios Arnonem, et aquae ductum fluviorum, qui declinavit usque ubi habitatur Ar, et sistit se ad terminum Moabi. Num.21:14,15.

Per Bella Jehovae in illo Verbo, sicut in nostro, intellectae et descriptae sunt pugnae Domini cum inferno et victoriae super illud, quando in mundum venturus esset. Eaedem etiam pugnae multis in locis intelliguntur et describuntur in historicis nostri Verbi, ut in bellis Josuae cum gentibus terrae Canaanis et in bellis Judicum et Regum Israelis.

Ex propheticis istius Verbi haec desumpta sunt a Mose,

Propterea dicunt **Enuntiatores**, Ingredimini Chesbonem; aedificabitur et confirmabitur urbs Sichonis. Nam ignis exivit ex Chesbone, flamma ex urbe Sichonis; comedit Ar Moabi, possessores excelsorum Arnonis. Vae tibi, Moabe; periisti, popule Kemoschi. Dedit filios suos evasores, et filias suas in captivitatem regi Emorraei Sichoni. Cum telis confecimus eos; periit Chesbon usque ad Dibonem, et devastavimus usque ad Nophach, quod usque ad Medebam. Num.21:27-30.

Translatores vertunt, **Proverbiorum Compositores**, sed vocandi **Enuntiatores** seu **Enuntiata Prophetica**, ut constare potest a significatione vocis **Moschalim** in lingua Hebraea, quod non modo sint proverbia sed etiam enuntiata prophetica, ut Num.23:7,18; 24:3,15, ubi dicitur quod Bileamus ediderit **enuntiatum suum**, quod fuit propheticum, etiam de Domino; enuntiatum ejus ibi vocatur Maschal in singulari. Accedit quod illa a Mose inde desumpta non sint proverbia sed prophetica. Quod illud Verbum similiter Divinum seu divinitus inspiratum fuerit, patet apud Jeremiam, ubi paene similia verba leguntur,

Ignis exivit ex Chesbone, et flamma ab inter Sichonem, quae comedit angulum Moabi, et verticem filiorum strepitus. Vae tibi, Moabe. Periit populus Kemoschi, nam rapti sunt filii tui in captivitatem, et filiae tuae in captivitatem. Jer.48:45,46.

Praeter illa nominatur etiam liber propheticus Verbi Vetusti vocatus Liber Jaschar, seu Liber Recti, a Davide et a Josua – a Davide,

    2   aquae ductum SS^1, *VR*: aquaeductum SS^2, SS^3
    3   ubi SS^3,*VR*: *om* SS^1, SS^2

Therefore it is said in **The Book of the Wars of Jehovah**, Vaheb in Suphah, and the rivers Arnon, and the water channel of the rivers, which went down even to where Ar is inhabited, and rested at the boundary of Moab. Num.21:14,15.

The Wars of Jehovah in that Word, as in ours, meant and described the Lord's conflicts with hell and His victories over it when He was to come into the world. The same conflicts too are meant and described in many places in the historical parts of our Word, as in Joshua's wars against the nations of the land of Canaan and in the wars of the Judges and Kings of Israel.

2   The following verses were taken by Moses from the prophetical parts of that Word,

Therefore **the Authors of Utterances** say, Come into Heshbon; the city of Sihon will be built and strengthened. For fire has gone forth from Heshbon, a flame from the city of Sihon. It has devoured Ar of Moab, those who possess the high places of Arnon. Woe to you, Moab; you are done for, people of Chemosh. He has made his sons fugitives, and his daughters captives of the Amorite king, Sihon. We have despatched them with arrows; Heshbon has perished as far as Dibon, and we have laid waste as far as Nophah, which is as far as Medeba. Num.21:27-30.

The translators render the phrase, **The Composers of Proverbs**, but it ought to be **The Authors of Utterances** or **The Prophetic Utterances**, as is evident from the meaning of the word **Moshalim** in the Hebrew language, that is, not only proverbs but also prophetic utterances, as at Num.23:7,18; 24:3,15. There it is said that Balaam gave forth **his utterance**, which was a prophecy, also about the Lord. His utterance is called Mashal in the singular. Furthermore, Moses' quotations from that source are not proverbs but prophecies. That Word was in a similar way Divine, that is, divinely inspired, as is plain from Jeremiah, where very similar words are written,

Fire has gone forth from Heshbon, and a flame from among Sihon, which has devoured the corner of Moab and the crown of the sons of noise. Woe to you, Moab; the people of Chemosh is done for, for your sons are taken into captivity, and your daughters into captivity. Jer.48:45,46.

In addition, a prophetical book of the old Word, called the Book of Jasher – that is, the Book of the Upright – is mentioned by David and Joshua. In the case of David,

Lamentatus est David super Schaule et super Jonathane; et inscripsit, Ad docendum filios Jehudae arcum. Ecce scripta super **Libro Jaschar**. 2 Sam.1:17,18.

Et a Josua,

5   Dixit Josua, Sol in Gibeone, quiesce, et luna in valle Ajalonis. Nonne hoc scriptum est super **Libro Jaschar**? Jos.10:12,13.

Insuper, dictum est mihi quod septem prima capita Geneseos in Verbo illo vetusto tam clare exstent ut non verbulum desit.

8   tam clare SS^3: *om* SS^1, SS^2

David made a lament for Saul and for Jonathan; and he wrote on it: For teaching the sons of Judah the bow. Behold, it is written in the **Book of Jasher**. 2 Sam.1:17,18.

And in the case of Joshua,

Joshua said, Be still, sun in Gibeon, and you, moon, in the valley of Aijalon. Is not this written in the **Book of Jasher**? Jos.10:12,13.

What is more, I have been told that the first seven chapters of Genesis are there in that old Word, so plainly[1] that not one small word is missing.

---

1   *so plainly* translates two words which do not appear in the first and second Latin editions, but in a parallel passage contained in a lengthy manuscript found among Swedenborg's possessions after his death. This manuscript is entitled **Diarium Spirituale** or, more recently, **Experientiae Spirituales**. An English translation of the parallel passage may be found in **On the Sacred Scripture or the Word of the Lord from Experience** published by the Swedenborg Society in 1997

Quod per Verbum etiam sit lux illis qui extra ecclesiam sunt et non habent Verbum

104 Non potest dari conjunctio cum caelo nisi alicubi in tellure sit ecclesia ubi est Verbum et per id Dominus notus, quia Dominus est Deus caeli et terrae, et absque Domino nulla salus. Satis est ut ecclesia sit ubi Verbum, tametsi illa consistit ex paucis respective; per id usque Dominus praesens est ubivis in universo terrarum orbe, nam per id caelum conjunctum est humano generi. Quod conjunctio sit per Verbum, videatur supra, n.62-69.

105 Quomodo autem praesentia et conjunctio Domini et caeli datur in omnibus terris per Verbum, dicetur. Universum caelum coram Domino est sicut unus homo, similiter ecclesia; quod etiam actualiter appareant ut homo, videatur in opere **De Caelo et Inferno**, n.59-86. In illo homine est ecclesia, ubi Verbum legitur et per id Dominus notus est, sicut **cor** et sicut **pulmo** – regnum caeleste ut cor et regnum spirituale ut pulmo. Sicut ex his binis fontibus vitae in humano corpore omnia reliqua membra et viscera subsistunt et vivunt, ita quoque omnes illi in terrarum orbe apud quos religiosum est, et Deus unus colitur et bene vivitur, et per id in homine illo sunt, et referunt membra et viscera ejus extra thoracem, ubi sunt cor et pulmo, ex conjunctione Domini et caeli per Verbum cum ecclesia, subsistunt et vivunt. Nam Verbum in ecclesia, tametsi est apud paucos respective, est vita reliquis a Domino per caelum, sicut membrorum et viscerum totius corporis est vita ex corde et pulmone; est quoque communicatio similis. Quae etiam causa est quod Christiani apud quos Verbum legitur constituant pectus illius hominis. Sunt etiam in medio omnium, et circum illos sunt Pontificii; circum hos sunt Mahumedani qui agnoscunt Dominum ut Maximum Prophetam ac ut Filium Dei. Post hos autem sunt Africani, ac

The Word also serves to enlighten those who are outside the church and do not possess the Word

104   There can be no link with heaven unless somewhere on earth there is a church which possesses the Word and so the Lord is known, because the Lord is the God of heaven and earth, and without the Lord there is no salvation. It is enough if there is a church which possesses the Word, even though it consists of relatively few people. The Lord is still present everywhere throughout the world, for it effects a link between heaven and the human race. For the link effected by the Word, see above, §§62-69.

105   But how the Lord and heaven are present in every land and linked to it by means of the Word must be explained. The whole of heaven is in the sight of the Lord like one person, and so is the church. They really look like a person, as may be seen in the work **Heaven and Hell**, §§59-86. That person contains the church, where the Word is read and so the Lord is known, just as the body contains a **heart** and **lungs**; the celestial kingdom serves as the heart and the spiritual kingdom as the lungs. Just as these two sources of life in the human body supply all the remaining limbs and organs with continued existence and life, so too the linking of the Lord and heaven with the church by means of the Word supplies continued existence and life to all those throughout the world who have a form of religion, worship one God, and lead a good life. Thus they form part of that person, and answer to the limbs and organs outside the chest where the heart and lungs reside. For the Word possessed by the church, though it exists with relatively few, is life to the remainder, supplied by the Lord through heaven, just as the life of the limbs and organs throughout the body comes from the heart and lungs. The communication between them too is similar. This too is why Christians who hear the Word read make up the chest of that person. They are also at the mid-most point of all, surrounded by the Roman Catholics; outside these come the Mohammedans who acknowledge the Lord as the Greatest Prophet and as the Son of God. After them come the Africans, and the outermost circumference

2

ultimam circumferentiam constituunt gentes et populi in Asia et in Indiis. De qua illorum ordinatione videantur aliqua in opusculo **De Ultimo Judicio**, n.48. Spectant etiam omnes, qui in homine illo sunt, versus meditullium, ubi sunt Christiani.

106 In meditullio, ubi sunt Christiani quibus est Verbum, est maxima lux, lux enim in caelis est Divinum Verum procedens a Domino ut sole ibi; et quia Verbum est illud, est maxima lux ubi sunt illi quibus est Verbum. Lux inde ut a suo centro se propagat circum in omnes peripherias usque ad ultimam; inde est illustratio gentium et populorum extra ecclesiam etiam per Verbum. Quod lux in caelis sit Divinum Verum procedens a Domino, et quod illa lux det intelligentiam non modo angelis sed etiam hominibus, videatur in opere **De Caelo et Inferno**, n.126-140.

107 Quod tale sit in universo caelo, concludi potest a simili in unaquavis societate ibi, nam unaquaevis societas caeli est caelum in minore forma, et quoque est sicut homo. Quod ita sit, videatur in opere **De Caelo et Inferno**, n.41-86. In omni societate caeli illi qui in medio ejus sunt, similiter referunt cor et pulmonem, et apud illos est maxima lux. Ipsa lux, et inde perceptio veri, a medio illo se propagat versus peripherias quaquaversum, ita ad omnes qui in societate sunt, et facit vitam illorum spiritualem. Ostensum est quod quando illi qui in medio erant – qui provinciam cordis et pulmonum constituebant et apud quos maxima lux erat – auferrentur, illi qui circum erant in umbra essent, et tunc in tam exili perceptione veri ut vix in aliqua; sed mox ut redierunt, visa est lux et fuit illis perceptio veri sicut prius.

108 Idem etiam illustrari potest ab hac experientia. Erant apud me spiritus Africani ex Abyssinia. Illis quondam aperiebantur aures, ut audirent cantum in aliquo templo in mundo ex Psalmo Davidis, ex quo afficiebantur tali jucunditate, ut una cum illis canerent. Sed mox claudebantur aures, ut non audirent inde aliquid; at tunc adhuc majore jucunditate afficiebantur, quia spirituali; et simul implebantur intelligentia, quia Psalmus ille agebat de Domino et de Redemptione. Causa crescentis jucunditatis erat quod illis data sit communicatio cum illa societate in caelo quae in conjunctione erat cum illis qui in mundo Psalmum illum canebant. Ex hac et pluri alia experientia, patuit quod communicatio cum universo caelo detur per Verbum. Propter

consists of nations and peoples in Asia and the Indies. Some details concerning this arrangement of all these people may be seen in the small work **The Last Judgment**, §48. All who are within that person look towards the centre where Christians are.

106 At the centre, where Christians are who possess the Word, there is the strongest light. In the heavens the light is Divine Truth emanating from the Lord as the sun there, and since the Word consists of that Truth the strongest light exists where those who possess the Word are. Light from it as its centre spreads to all surrounding areas right out to the last, and therefore nations and peoples outside the church too are enlightened by means of the Word. Regarding light in the heavens being Divine Truth emanating from the Lord, and the giving of intelligence by that light to people as well as angels, see the work **Heaven and Hell**, §§126-140.

107 It can be deduced that all this is so in the whole of heaven from the similar situation to be found in each community there, for each community in heaven is a heaven on a smaller scale, also resembling a person, as may be seen in the work **Heaven and Hell**, §§41-86. In every community in heaven those who are at the centre in a similar way answer to the heart and lungs, and they enjoy the strongest light. The light itself, and consequently the perception of truth, spreads from the centre in all directions towards the circumference, thus reaching all members of the community and bringing them spiritual life. A demonstration showed that on the removal of these at the centre, who made up the province of the heart and the lungs and enjoyed the strongest light, the surrounding people were then in the dark and had such a tenuous perception of truth as to be scarcely any at all. But as soon as those at the centre returned, they saw the light, and their perception of truth was as before.

108 The following experience when African spirits from Abyssinia were present with me may also serve to show the same thing. At some point their ears were opened so that they might hear the singing in some church in the world of a Psalm of David. They were so delighted with this singing that they joined in with it. But soon their ears were closed so that they heard nothing at all from that church; yet they experienced even greater delight, because this was spiritual, and at the same time they were filled with understanding, because the Lord and Redemption were the theme of that psalm. They experienced this increase of delight because they were brought into connection with that community in heaven which was linked to the people in the world singing that psalm. This experience and many others have made it plain to me that a link to the whole of

illam causam, ex Divina Domini providentia, commercium universale regnorum Europae, principaliter illorum ubi Verbum legitur, est cum gentibus extra ecclesiam.

109 Comparatio fieri potest cum calore et luce ex sole mundi, quae vegetationem dant arboribus et virgultis, etiam illis quae ad latera et quae sub nube stant, modo sol ortus sit et in mundo appareat. Ita lux et calor caeli a Domino ut sole, quae lux est Divinum Verum, ex quo omnis intelligentia et sapientia est angelis et hominibus. Quare dicitur de Verbo quod erat apud Deum, et erat Deus, quod illuminet omnem hominem venientem in mundum, Joh.1:1,9, et quod lux illa etiam in tenebris appareat, vers.5.

110 Ex his constare potest quod Verbum, quod est in Ecclesia Reformatorum, illustret omnes gentes et populos per communicationem spiritualem, tum quod provideatur a Domino ut in tellure semper sit ecclesia, ubi Verbum legitur et per id Dominus notus est. Quare cum Verbum a Pontificiis paene rejectum erat, ex Divina Domini providentia facta est Reformatio, et inde Verbum iterum receptum est, et quoque quod sanctum habeatur Verbum a nobili gente inter Pontificios.

111 Quoniam absque Verbo non est cognitio Domini, ita non salvatio, ideo quando Verbum apud gentem Judaicam prorsus falsificatum et adulteratum erat, et inde quasi nullum factum est, tunc placuit Domino e caelo descendere, et venire in mundum, ac implere Verbum, et per id redintegrare et restituere illud, ac iterum dare lucem incolis telluris, secundum Domini verba,

Populus sedens in tenebris vidit lumen magnum, sedentibus in regione et umbra mortis, lux exorta illis est. Matt.4:16; Esai.9:1.

112 Quoniam praedictum est quod in fine hujus ecclesiae etiam oborirentur tenebrae ex non cognitione et agnitione Domini quod sit Deus caeli et terrae, et ex fidei separatione a charitate, ne per id genuinus intellectus Verbi periret, ideo

---

5 dant *VR*: dat *SS*

heaven is brought about by means of the Word. For this reason countries in Europe, chiefly those in which people read the Word, are in the Lord's Divine providence in general contact with nations outside the church.

109 This may be compared with heat and light coming from the sun of the world, which give trees and plants the power to grow, even if they are placed to one side or are under a cloud, provided that the sun has risen and is shining on the world. The same is true of the light and heat in heaven flowing from the Lord as the sun there. This light is Divine Truth, the source of all intelligence and wisdom for angels in heaven as well as people on earth. This is why it is said of the Word that it was with God and was God, that it enlightens everyone who comes into the world, John 1:1,9, and that the light also shines in the darkness, verse 5.

110 These facts may establish that the Word which exists in the Church of the Reformed is the source of enlightenment to all nations and peoples by means of spiritual communication. They also show that the Lord ensures that on earth there always exists a church in which the Word is read and through it the Lord is known. Therefore when the Word was more or less rejected by the Roman Catholics, in the Lord's Divine providence the Reformation took place and as a result the Word was accepted once again, and in addition was taken to be holy by an admirable nation[1] among the Roman Catholics.

111 Because without the Word there is no knowledge of the Lord, nor thus any salvation, when the Word possessed by the Jewish nation was utterly falsified and adulterated, so that it was consequently made practically null, it therefore pleased the Lord to come down from heaven, and into the world, to fulfil the Word, and in so doing to renew and restore it, and give light again to the inhabitants of the earth, as these words of the Lord declare,

The people sitting in darkness have seen a great light; for those sitting in the region and shadow of death, upon them has a light dawned. Matt.4:16; Isa.9:2.

112 It has been predicted that at the end of the present church too darkness will arise, due to its failure to know and accept that the Lord is the God of heaven and earth, and due to the separation of faith from charity. But so that this should not result in the loss of a

---

1 ie the French nation after the Reformation (and before the Revolution of 1789 onwards)

placuit Domino nunc revelare sensum spiritualem Verbi, et manifestare quod Verbum in illo sensu, et ex illo in sensu naturali, agat de Domino et de ecclesia, imo de illis solis, et plura alia per quae lux veri ex Verbo, paene exstincta, restituatur. Quod lux veri in fine hujus ecclesiae paene exstincta esset, praedicitur multis in locis in Apocalypsi, et quoque intelligitur per haec Domini verba apud Matthaeum,

Statim post afflictionem dierum istorum sol obscurabitur, et luna non dabit lumen suum, et stellae cadent de caelo, et virtutes caelorum commovebuntur. Et tunc videbunt Filium Hominis venientem in nubibus caeli cum virtute et gloria. Matt.24:29,30.

Per solem ibi intelligitur Dominus quoad amorem, per lunam Dominus quoad fidem, per stellas Dominus quoad cognitiones boni et veri, per Filium Hominis Dominus quoad Verbum, per nubem sensus literae Verbi, et per gloriam sensus spiritualis ac transparentia ejus in sensu literae.

113 Per multam experientiam mihi scire datum est quod per Verbum sit homini communicatio cum caelo. Dum perlegi Verbum a primo capite Esaiae usque ad ultimum Malachiae, et Psalmos Davidis, datum est clare percipere quod unusquisque versus communicaret cum aliqua societate caeli et quod sic totum Verbum cum universo caelo.

---

11   virtute et gloria: gloria et virtute *SS, VR*

genuine understanding of the Word, it has now pleased the Lord to reveal its spiritual sense, and to demonstrate that the Word in that sense, and from this in the natural sense, has to do with the Lord and the church, indeed with these alone, and to demonstrate much else whereby the light of truth coming from the Word, which is almost extinguished, may be restored. Many places in the Book of Revelation predict that the light of truth would be almost extinguished at the end of the present church, and this too is the meaning of these words of the Lord in Matthew,

Immediately after the affliction of those days the sun will be darkened, and the moon will not give its light, and the stars will fall from the sky, and the powers of the heavens will be shaken. And then they will see the Son of Man coming in the clouds of heaven with power and glory. Matt.24:29,30.

The sun there means the Lord in respect of love, the moon the Lord in respect of faith, the stars the Lord in respect of knowledge of goodness and truth, the Son of Man the Lord in respect of the Word, cloud the literal sense of the Word, and glory the spiritual sense and the way it is visible within the literal sense.

113   By repeated experience I have been granted the knowledge that the Word provides a person with a means of communication with heaven. When I read through the Word from the first chapter of Isaiah to the end of Malachi, and also the Psalms of David, I was granted a clear perception that each verse communicated with some community in heaven, and that thus the entire Word communicated with heaven as a whole.[1]

---

1   See page ix of the Editor and Translator's Introduction to **DD**, referred to above, in the footnote on page 145

Quod nisi Verbum foret, nemo sciret Deum, caelum et infernum, vitam post mortem, et minus Dominum

114 Hoc ut commune conclusum sequitur ex omnibus quae hactenus dicta et ostensa sunt, ut,

Quod Verbum sit ipsum Divinum Verum, n.1-4
Quod Verbum sit medium conjunctionis cum angelis caeli, n.62-69
Quod in Verbo ubivis sit conjugium Domini et ecclesiae, et inde conjugium boni et veri, n.80-89
Quod ecclesia talis sit, qualis est intellectus Verbi ab illa, n.76-79
Quod Verbum etiam in caelis sit, et quod ex illo angelis sapientia, n.70-75
Quod etiam sit lux spiritualis gentibus et populis extra ecclesiam per Verbum, n.104-113
Praeter plura.

Ex quibus concludi potest quod absque Verbo non alicui sit intelligentia spiritualis, quae est, quod sciat Deum, caelum et infernum, et vitam post mortem, et prorsus non aliquid sciat de Domino, de fide et amore in Ipsum, ita non aliquid de redemptione, per quam tamen salvatio. Dicit etiam Dominus ad discipulos,

Sine Me non potestis facere quicquam. Joh.15:5.

Et Johannes,

Non potest homo sumere quicquam nisi sit datum illi e caelo. Joh.3:27.

115 Sed quia illi qui statuunt, et apud se confirmaverunt, quod homo absque Verbo scire posset existentiam Dei, et quoque caeli et inferni, tum aliquid de reliquis quae

If the Word did not exist no one would know of the existence of God, heaven and hell, and life after death, even less of the Lord

114   This follows as the general conclusion drawn from all that has been stated and demonstrated so far, from, for instance –

The Word is Divine Truth itself, §§1-4.
The Word produces a link with the angels in heaven, §§62-69.
The Word in every part contains a marriage of the Lord and the church, and so a marriage of goodness and truth, §§80-89.
What the church is like depends on how the Word is understood by it, §§76-79.
The Word is to be found also in the heavens and is the source of angels' wisdom, §§70-75.
Also, nations and peoples outside the church receive spiritual light through the Word, §§104-113.
And much more.

All this may lead to the conclusion that without the Word no one possesses any spiritual understanding, which consists in knowing of the existence of God, heaven and hell, and life after death. They would not know anything at all about the Lord, believing in and loving Him, and so not a thing about redemption, when yet this is the way to salvation. Also the Lord tells His disciples,

Without Me you can do nothing. John 15:5.

And John says,

People cannot receive anything unless it is given them from heaven. John 3:27.

115   But since those who decide and have proved to themselves that without the Word a person could know of the existence of God, and also of heaven and hell, as well as anything among all the

Verbum docet, et illi per id auctoritatem et sanctitatem Verbi infirmant, si non ore usque corde, ideo non licet cum illis ex Verbo agere, sed ex lumine rationali. Nam non credunt Verbo sed sibi. Ex lumine rationali inquire, et invenies quod duae facultates vitae sint apud hominem, quae vocantur intellectus et voluntas, et quod intellectus subjectus sit voluntati, et non voluntas intellectui, intellectus enim solum docet et monstrat viam. Inquire etiam, et invenies quod voluntas hominis sit ejus proprium, et quod hoc in se spectatum sit mere malum, et quod inde sit falsum in intellectu.

Quum haec inveneris, videbis quod homo ex se non velit aliud intelligere quam quod est ex proprio voluntatis ejus, et quod nec possit, nisi alibi sit unde id sciat. Homo ex proprio voluntatis suae non vult aliud intelligere quam quod sui et mundi est; quicquid supra est, ei in caligine est. Ut dum videt solem, lunam, et stellas, si tunc forte cogitaret de ortu illorum, non aliter posset cogitare quam quod illa a se sint. Num altius quam plures docti in mundo, qui tametsi sciunt ex Verbo creationem omnium a Deo, usque agnoscunt naturam? Quid tunc iidem si nihil ex Verbo scivissent? Num credis quod veteres sophi, ac Aristoteles, Cicero, Seneca, et alii, qui de Deo et de immortalitate animae scripserunt, id primum ex proprio sumserint? Non, sed ex aliis qui per traducem ex illis qui id primum sciverunt ex Verbo Vetusto. Scriptores theologiae naturalis nec hauriunt quicquam tale ex se; sed modo confirmant illa quae sciunt ab ecclesia, in qua est Verbum, per rationalia; et possunt dari inter illos qui confirmant et tamen non credunt.

116   Datum est videre populos in insulis natos, quoad civilia rationales, qui ne hilum sciverunt de Deo. Illi in mundo spirituali apparent sicut simiae, ac paene simili vita cum illis. At quia homines nati sunt, et inde in facultate recipiendi vitam spiritualem, instruuntur ab angelis, et per cognitiones de Domino ut Homine vivificantur. Qualis est homo ex se, apparet evidenter ex illis qui in inferno sunt, inter quos etiam

17   non *VR*: num *SS*
21   ac *SS*: ut *VR*
24   Vetusto *SS*[3], *VR*: *om SS*[1], *SS*[2]

rest that the Word teaches, and who thereby belittle the authority and holiness of the Word, if not with their lips yet in their heart, it is not possible to argue with them from the Word, only from the enlightenment of reason. For they do not believe the Word, only themselves. Use the enlightenment of reason to enquire into it, and you will find that a person has two faculties of life, called the understanding and the will, and that the understanding is subject to the will, and not the will to the understanding. For the understanding simply shows and indicates the way to go. Enquire again and you will find that people's will is their self, and that the self is essentially evil, and the source of false ideas in the understanding.

When you have reached these conclusions you will see that people left to themselves are unwilling to grasp anything intellectually that is not from the self in their will; nor can they do anything but this if they have no other source for that knowledge. From the self in their will people are unwilling to grasp anything intellectually other than selfish and worldly interests. Anything above this level is shrouded in thick darkness. For instance, when they look upon the sun, the moon, and the stars, if they happen to think about the origin of these, they can only suppose that they arose by themselves. Is this thinking any deeper than that of many experts in the world, who despite knowing from the Word that all things were created by God still attribute their origin to nature? What then would these same people think if they had learned nothing from the Word? Do you believe that the sages of old, and Aristotle, Cicero, Seneca, and others, who wrote about God and the immortality of the soul, got this idea first from their self? No, they got it from others who in turn received it from what had come down to them from those who knew it first from the Word of old. Nor do the writers on natural theology draw any such ideas from themselves; rather, they merely support by rational arguments what they learn from the church, which possesses the Word. There may too be those among them who support these ideas without actually believing them.

116 I have been allowed to see peoples born in the islands,[1] who had reasonable ideas of civil life, yet were totally ignorant about God. In the spiritual world they look like monkeys and live almost like these. But because they were born human beings, and consequently have the faculty of receiving spiritual life, they are taught by angels and endowed with life by learning about the Lord as being Human. What people are like left to themselves is plainly

---

1   ie of the Pacific

aliqui antistites et eruditi sunt qui ne quidem volunt audire de Deo, et propterea nec possunt nominare Deum. Hos vidi, et cum illis loquutus sum; et quoque loquutus sum cum illis qui in ignem irae et excandescentiae venerunt, cum audiverunt aliquem loquentem de Deo. Expende itaque, qualis homo foret qui nihil audivit de Deo, cum quidam tales sunt qui audiverunt de Deo, scripserunt de Deo, et praedicaverunt de Deo; sunt plures tales ex Jesuitis. Quod tales sint, est ex voluntate quae mala est, et haec, ut prius dictum est, ducit intellectum et aufert verum quod ibi est ex Verbo. Si homo ex se potuisset scire quod Deus sit et quod vita post mortem, cur non sciverat quod homo sit homo post mortem? Cur credit quod anima seu spiritus ejus sit sicut ventus aut sicut aether, qui non videt oculis, et audit auribus, et loquitur ore, priusquam conjungitur et coalescit cum suo cadavere et cum suo sceleto?

Pone itaque doctrinam pro cultu ex solo lumine rationali exclusam, annon foret ut ipse coleretur? ut factum est a saeculis et hodie fit ab illis qui sciunt ex Verbo quod solus Deus colendus sit. Cultus alius ex proprio hominis non dari potest, ne quidem cultus solis et lunae.

117   Quod ab antiquissimis temporibus fuerit religio, et incolae orbis ubivis noverint de Deo, et aliquid de vita post mortem, non fuit ex ipsis, et ex proprio illorum acumine, sed ex Verbo Vetusto, de quo supra, n.101-103, et postea ex Verbo Israelitico. Ex his religiosa emanaverunt in Indias et illarum insulas perque Aegyptum ac Aethiopiam in regna Africae, et ex maritimis Asiae in Graeciam, et inde in Italiam. Sed quia Verbum non potuit aliter quam per repraesentativa esse conscriptum, quae sunt talia in mundo quae correspondent caelestibus et inde significant illa, ideo religiosa plurium gentium versa sunt in idololatrica, et in Graecia in fabulosa; ac attributa et praedicata Divina in totidem deos, quibus praefecerunt supremum, quem vocaverunt Jovem, forte a Jehovah. Quod illis cognitio fuerit de paradiso, de diluvio, de igne sacro, de quatuor aetatibus, a prima aurea ad ultimam ferream, per quas in Verbo significantur quatuor status ecclesiae, ut apud Danielem 2:31-35, notum est. Quod

32   idololatrica SS^1, SS^2: idolatrica SS^3
34   forte SS^3, VR: om SS^1, SS^2

to be seen by considering those in hell, who include some leaders of the church and scholars. These are not even willing to listen to anything about God, and therefore neither can they name God. I have seen these people and talked to them. I have also talked to people who became fired with anger and wrath when they heard anyone speaking about God. Imagine therefore what someone who has heard nothing about God is going to be like when this is the nature of certain people who have heard about God, written about God, and preached about God. Very many such as these belong to the Jesuits. Their nature is the result of a will that is evil, and the will, as said before, guides the understanding and carries away the truth that is there, derived from the Word.

If people could know by themselves that God exists and there is life after death, why would they not know that a person remains a person after death? Why do they believe that a person's soul, that is, spirit, is like wind or like ether, with no eyes to see, no ears to hear, and no mouth to speak with, until it is joined to and coalesces with the person's corpse or skeleton?

Suppose then a teaching to do with worship that was hatched from nothing but the light of reason – would it not prescribe the worship of oneself? That is what has happened for ages, and what is done today by people who have learned from the Word that God alone is to be worshipped. No other kind of worship could exist based upon the human self, not even a worship of the sun and the moon.

117 Religion existed from most ancient times, and the inhabitants of all parts of the world knew about God, and something about life after death. This knowledge did not come from them themselves or their own intelligence but from the Word of old, described above, §§101-103, and later on from the Israelite Word. Religious beliefs based upon these two Words spread to the Indies and adjacent islands, and by way of Egypt and Ethiopia to the kingdoms of Africa, and from the coasts of Asia to Greece, and from there to Italy. But because the Word could not have been written other than by means of representatives, which are the sort of things in the world that correspond to heavenly things and so stand for them, the religious beliefs of many nations turned into forms of idolatry, and in Greece into fables. The attributes and qualities of God became so many gods, and they set over them the highest whom they called Jove, perhaps after Jehovah. It is well known that they knew about paradise, the flood, the sacred fire, and the four ages, beginning with the golden and ending with the iron age, which in the Word stand for four states of the church, as in Daniel 2:31-5. It is also well known

religiosum Mahumedanum, quod successit, et religiosa plurium gentium priora delevit, ex Verbo utriusque Testamenti desumptum sit, etiam notum est.

118 Ultimo dicam quales illi post mortem fiunt qui propriae intelligentiae omnia adscribunt ac parum, si quicquam, Verbo. Primum fiunt sicut ebrii, postea sicut fatui, et demum stupidi, et sedent in tenebris. Caveant itaque sibi a tali delirio.

that the Muslim religion which followed, and which wiped out the previous religious systems of many nations, drew on the Word in both Testaments.

118 Finally let me describe what happens after death to those who attribute everything to their own intelligence and little, if anything, to the Word. First of all they become as if drunk, then as if out of their minds, and finally idiots, sitting in darkness. Let them beware therefore of such madness.

TABLE OF PARALLEL PASSAGES

SS	VR	SS	VR
1-4	VR 189-192	66	VR 237
5-6	VR 194-195	67	VR 236
9-10	VR 196-197	68-69	VR 239
14	VR 198	70-72	VR 240-241
17	VR 199	73-75	VR 242
18	VR 200	76	VR 243
20-21	VR 201-202	79	VR 247
22-23	VR 204-205	80-81	VR 248
24-25	VR 206-207	82-83	VR 249
26	VR 208, 277	84	VR 250
	AR 255	86	VR 251
27-28	VR 210	87-88	VR 252-253
29	VR 211	90	VR 278
33	VR 213	91-92	VR 254
37-39	VR 214	93-94	VR 255-256
40-41	VR 215	95	VR 257
42	VR 216	96	VR 258
43	VR 217	96A	VR 259
44-48	VR 218-222	97	VR 260
49:3,4	VR 223	98	VR 261
50-51	VR 225-226	99	VR 109
52	VR 228	100	VR 263
53	VR 229	101	VR 264
55	VR 229	102	VR 279
56	VR 230	103	VR 265
57-58	VR 231	104-105	VR 267-268
60	VR 232	107,109	VR 269
61	VR 233	110-111	VR 270
	AR 255	112-113	VR 271-272
62-63	VR 234	115	VR 273
64	VR 235	116-118	VR 274-276